The Law Commission
Consultation Paper No 160

THE ILLEGALITY DEFENCE IN TORT

A Consultation Paper

London: The Stationery Office

Applications for reproduction should be made in writing to
The Copyright Unit, Her Majesty's Stationery Office,
St. Clements House, 2-16 Colegate, Norwich NR3 1BQ

ISBN 0 11 730245 7

Printed in the United Kingdom for The Stationery Office
TJ4707 C12 6/01 19585

Hugh Beale

Our Reference: 30-188-02

Your Reference:

LAW COMMISSION
CONQUEST HOUSE
37/38 JOHN STREET
THEOBALDS ROAD
LONDON WC1N 2BQ

TEL: 020-7453-1216

FAX: 020-7453-1297

hugh.beale@lawcommission.gsi.gov.uk

27 June 2001

Professor J C Steele
Lecturer in Law
Faculty of Law
University of Southampton
Highfield
Southampton
SO9 5NH

Dear Jennifer

CONSULTATION PAPER NO 160: THE ILLEGALITY DEFENCE IN TORT

The Law Commission has just published Consultation Paper No 160: *The Illegality Defence in Tort*. In brief, the paper considers whether a claimant's illegal conduct can amount to a defence to an action in tort, and makes provisional proposals for reform of the law. I have pleasure in enclosing a copy of the paper in the hope that you will find it of interest and that you will let us have comments on it.

This paper is related to Consultation Paper No 154: *Illegal Transactions: the Effect of Illegality on Contracts and Trusts*, which we published early in 1999. Following the consultation process for Consultation Paper No 160 it is likely that we will publish one final report in respect of the areas covered by both Consultation Paper No 160 and Consultation Paper No 154.

The closing date for receipt of comments is 28 September 2001. You may send your comments to me or to the lawyer responsible for the project. Until 31 July, this will be James Robinson; from 1 August the project will be taken over by Helen Hall (contact details are given on the inside front cover of the paper).

I hope that you will be able to respond to this consultation paper, and we look forward to hearing from you.

Yours sincerely,

Hugh Beale
Commissioner, Common Law

30-188-04

THE LAW COMMISSION

THE ILLEGALITY DEFENCE IN TORT

CONTENTS

iv

TABLE OF CASES

PART I
INTRODUCTION

1. THE AIM OF THIS PAPER

1.1 In 1999 we published Consultation Paper No 154, Illegal Transactions: the Effect of Illegality on Contracts and Trusts.[1] In that paper we considered the law relating to the doctrine of illegality as it operated in contract and trusts, and proposed that the current rules-based approach should be reformed by the introduction of a statutory discretion, structured around a number of factors. In the consultation paper we stated that we did not propose to address the question of illegality as it operated in tort.[2] We considered that tort gave rise to different issues from those raised by contract and trusts, and we were not aware that the area was one that gave rise to concern.

1.2 We received just over fifty responses from individuals, institutions and organisations. One of our questions was whether consultees agreed with our provisional view that the law relating to illegality in contract and trusts is in need of reform, and that legislative reform is to be preferred to judicially-based reform of the common law. Of those who gave a clear response to this question (thirty seven consultees), the vast majority agreed with our provisional view. There was broad support for our provisional proposal to introduce a structured discretion to replace the current rules. We are considering our proposed reforms to the law relating to contract and trusts in the light of these responses, but it is likely that our final report will recommend the adoption of some form of structured discretionary regime.

1.3 Several of those who responded to the consultation paper questioned whether it was appropriate to omit tort from the scope of our consideration and the consultation process. The broad thrust of the comments was that it would be desirable to have the same principles relating to illegality applying in all branches of the law, to prevent what would be seen as the odd situation of having a carefully structured discretion for contract and trusts law but leaving tortious remedies subject to the perceived uncertainties of the concept of *ex turpi causa non oritur actio*.[3] Since the publication of the consultation paper we have also had our own misgivings about this omission. In the light of both consultees' and our own concerns we decided to extend our examination of the law to consider the effects of the illegality doctrine as it operates in tort.

1.4 Our change of view as to the appropriateness of including tort within the scope of the project has been prompted by two main factors. First, we appreciate the comments made by some consultees about the inconsistency that would arise as between our provisional proposals for legislative reform in contract and trusts and

---

[1] Below we refer to this as the "consultation paper" or "Consultation Paper No 154".

[2] Consultation Paper No 154, para 1.3.

[3] We explain the operation of this doctrine later in this paper. See below, Part II.

the common law of tort, were we to exclude consideration of tort. We think that there is particular force in this point where there are concurrent or parallel claims in contract and tort (for example, a claim for breach of contract coupled with a claim for fraudulent misrepresentation or an alternative claim in conversion). If our provisional proposals for contract and trusts were to be implemented, but the defence in tort left untouched, a court might be required to apply both a statutory discretion and a series of common law rules in relation to the same illegal conduct in the same case, depending on which cause of action it was considering.[4] We do not think this outcome would fulfil our statutory duty to work towards the "systematic development and reform" of the law.[5] Secondly, a number of important tort cases have been reported since the decision was taken to exclude tort from the scope of Consultation Paper No 154. Some of these cases are potentially controversial, and merit examination.

1.5 In addition, an important point we raise at this stage is that the problems with the clarity of the current law - which we discuss in Parts II, IV and V - mean that it is difficult to predict an outcome or to explain the outcome in terms of the apparent rationale for the illegality defence, with the result that there is a risk of arbitrariness or possibly disproportionality. Arbitrary or disproportionate results could lead to conflict with the European Convention on Human Rights (ECHR):

> In a democratic society subscribing to the rule of law, no determination that is arbitrary can ever be regarded as lawful.[6]

1.6 Proportionality is also a fundamental principle in ECHR jurisprudence.[7] Lester and Pannick[8] suggest that:

> Interpretation of the Human Rights Act should strive to give effect to the general principle, 'inherent in the whole of the Convention', that it is seeking to strike a 'fair balance...between the demands of the general interest of the community and the requirements of the protection of the individual's fundamental rights'.[9]

They go on to state:[10]

> Central to the principle of a 'fair balance' is the doctrine of proportionality. A restriction on a freedom guaranteed by the

---

[4] See below, paras 5.9-5.11.

[5] See Law Commissions Act 1965, s 3. See below, para 5.12 n 16.

[6] *Winterwerp v Netherlands* (1979) 2 EHRR 387, para 39. See Lord Lester of Herne Hill and D Pannick (ed), *Human Rights Law and Practice* (1999) para 4.19.20.

[7] See Consultation Paper No 154, para 1.23. See also R Clayton and H Tomlinson, *The Law of Human Rights* (2000) vol 1, paras 6.40-6.85, and K Starmer, *European Human Rights Law* (1999) paras 4.37 ff.

[8] Lord Lester of Herne Hill and D Pannick (ed), *Human Rights Law and Practice* (1999).

[9] *Ibid*, at para 3.09 (footnotes omitted). *Sporrong and Lönnroth v Sweden* (1982) 5 EHRR 35, 52 and *Soering v United Kingdom* (1989) 11 EHRR 439, 468 are cited.

[10] *Ibid*, at para 3.10.

Convention must be 'proportionate to the legitimate aim pursued'.[11] There must be 'a reasonable relationship of proportionality between the means employed and the legitimate objectives pursued by the contested limitation'.[12]

1.7   A measure will satisfy the proportionality test only if three criteria are satisfied. The legislative objective must be sufficiently important to justify limiting a fundamental right; the measures designed to meet that objective must not be arbitrary, unfair or based on irrational considerations, and the means used to impair the right or freedom must be no more than are necessary to accomplish the legitimate objective: the more severe the deleterious effects of the measure, the more important the objective must be if it is to be justified.[13]

1.8   We believe that the increased importance given to the ECHR by virtue of the Human Rights Act 1998 reinforces the need to tie decisions more closely to the policy rationales that underlie the illegality doctrine, particularly given the principle of proportionality. It has already been suggested by one academic commentator that the rule stated in one of the cases, *Clunis v Camden and Islington Health Authority*,[14] if applied in a blanket way, might be in violation of Article 2 of the ECHR to the extent that the illegality defence is applied to bar a claim by the claimant or his or her dependants stemming from conduct taking or endangering his or her life.[15] There may be other examples. For instance, unpredictable or arbitrary use of the illegality doctrine to bar an action for conversion[16] might conflict with Article 1 of the First Protocol to the ECHR (the right to property).[17]

---

[11]   *Handyside v United Kingdom* (1976) 1 EHRR 737, 754 (footnote in original).

[12]   *Fayed v United Kingdom* (1994) 18 EHRR 393, 432 (footnote in original).

[13]   Lord Lester of Herne Hill and D Pannick (ed), *Human Rights Law and Practice* (1999), para 3.10.

[14]   [1998] QB 978. See below, para 2.7.

[15]   See *Clerk and Lindsell on Torts* (18th ed 2000) para 1-71.

[16]   We question whether the concept of "reliance" on the illegal conduct could be arbitrary. See below, para 5.35.

[17]   See, eg, R Clayton and H Tomlinson, *The Law of Human Rights* (2000) vol 1, ch 18. An interference with property must satisfy the requirement of proportionality (as well as being in the public or general interest). There must also be legal certainty; see Lord Lester of Herne Hill and D Pannick (ed), *Human Rights Law and Practice* (1999) para 4.19.20:

> Legal certainty requires the existence of and compliance with adequately accessible and sufficiently precise domestic legal provisions, which satisfy the essential requirements of the concept of 'law'.

See also *ibid*, at para 4.19.21:

> There must also be procedural safeguards against the misuse of powers of the State. For example, in *Hentrich v France* [(1994) 18 EHRR 440], concerning the pre-emption of the applicant's property by the French revenue authorities, the E Ct HR held that the principle of legality had been breached because the pre-emption *'operated arbitrarily and selectively and was scarcely foreseeable, and it was not attended by the basic procedural safeguards'*. (Emphasis added).

For a recent example of a case in which the Court of Appeal has considered a submission that the use of the illegality defence contravened Article 1 of the First Protocol, see *Al-*

1.9 This need for a clear link between the use of the illegality doctrine and the policies that underlie it caused us to re-examine those policies as part of our consideration of the law.[18] We have some doubts as to whether the policy rationales that had previously been examined in the consultation paper are always appropriate or adequate in their explanatory power, particularly when applied to tort. This aspect is considered further in Part IV of this paper.

1.10 On 22 March 2001 we held a seminar on "The Illegality Defence in Tort" at the Institute of Advanced Legal Studies in London, which we had organised jointly with the Society for Advanced Legal Studies and the Tort Section of the Society of Public Teachers of Law.[19] Prior to this seminar we had produced a draft version of this consultation paper which we circulated to those attending, as well as to other interested parties. The seminar was chaired by Professor Hugh Beale, one of the Law Commissioners, and the speakers were Lord Justice Mummery and Professor Michael Jones. The seminar took the form of a discussion of the draft version of this consultation paper. We are grateful to those who attended this seminar, and to those who gave us comments on the draft paper. In writing this final version we have taken account of the main issues raised and discussed in this seminar, as well as a number of other comments received about the draft from persons who were invited to the seminar but were unable to attend.

2. STRUCTURE OF THE PAPER

1.11 Following this Introduction, in Part II of this paper we review the doctrine of illegality as it currently affects claims in tort in England and Wales. In Part III we consider how the doctrine has operated in a number of other jurisdictions; we include this section because it has helped to inform our proposals for reform in our own jurisdiction. In Part IV we reappraise the policies that lie behind the doctrine both in tort and more generally. In Part V we consider whether reform is necessary, and conclude that it is necessary, or at least advantageous, to remedy what we perceive as problems with the current operation of the law, as well as for purposes of clarity and consistency. In Part VI we set out our provisional proposals for reform of this area, which, as with contract and trusts, consist of the introduction of a structured statutory discretion. In Part VII, we summarise our provisional proposals and the issues on which we invite responses. Finally,

---

Kishtaini v Shanshal, The Times 8 March 2001. The illegality in this case concerned the transfer of money in breach of Directions made in implementation of United Nations sanctions against Iraq. Argument on compatibility with the First Protocol focused on the "public interest" exception, and it was held that there was no inconsistency with the ECHR given that:

> [t]he Directions embody a very high public interest originating in the resolutions of the Security Council of the United Nations in an international emergency. (*per* Mummery LJ, from transcript).

In addition, the necessary proportionality and fair balance between the public interest and private right was afforded by the machinery for the claimant to apply to the Bank of England for permission to carry out the transaction in question.

[18] We had examined the policies in the context of contract and trusts in Part VI of Consultation Paper No 154.

[19] Below we refer to this seminar as the "consultation seminar".

Appendix A reproduces the summary of recommendations and consultation issues from Consultation Paper No 154, and Appendix B provides a select bibliography.

3. THE MEANING OF "ILLEGALITY"

1.12 One important point that needs to be considered is what we mean by "illegality". A Latin phrase that has often featured in cases involving a claimant who has acted in an illegal manner (particularly in tort cases) is *ex turpi causa non oritur actio*.[20] The appropriateness of this phrase has been questioned both by judges and by academic commentators.[21] Other Latin phrases have been used in this context.[22] As to the meaning of "illegal conduct" in tort, it seems to us that there are three possible interpretations. One would restrict the use of the phrase to those actions that were in breach of the criminal law; another would be to include both criminal actions and those that were in breach of the civil law, and a third would be to include criminal wrongs, civil wrongs, and immoral behaviour.

1.13 When we discussed what was meant by "illegal transaction" for the purposes of Consultation Paper No 154, we found this to be a difficult question to answer.[23] We were of the opinion that it would be too limited a view to restrict the meaning of "illegal transaction" to those transactions where the formation, purpose or performance involved the commission of a legal wrong, and took as the broad remit both this situation and conduct which was "otherwise contrary to public policy".[24] This public policy side of illegality is more likely to be of importance in claims involving contracts or trusts than tort, although those tort claims which can be seen as parasitic on a contract may fall within this head.

1.14 It can be seen from the comments made by judges that the operation of the illegality doctrine in tort cases is not confined to criminal illegality, but in principle can include other reprehensible or grossly immoral conduct.[25] However, with the exception of one case, we have not been able to find an example of

---

[20] See below, para 2.1.

[21] See, eg, the comments made in *Pitts v Hunt* [1991] 1 QB 24:

> I find the ritual incantation of the maxim *ex turpi causa non oritur actio* more likely to confuse than to illuminate. (*per* Balcombe LJ *ibid*, at p 49).

> That a defence of illegality can be pleaded to a case founded in tort is...clear, whether or not the defence is correctly called *ex turpi causa*. (*per* Dillon LJ *ibid*, at p 57).

> See also N Enonchong, *Illegal Transactions* (1998) pp 94-95.

[22] Eg, Lord Mansfield uses the phrase *ex dolo malo non oritur actio* in *Holman v Johnson* (1775) 1 Cowp 341, 343; 98 ER 1120, 1121.

[23] See Consultation Paper No 154, para 1.4.

[24] See *ibid*, paras 1.4-1.11 for a full discussion of the concept of "illegal transaction".

[25] See, eg, the comments of Kerr LJ in *Euro-Diam Ltd v Bathurst* [1990] 1 QB 1, 35, cited by Lloyd LJ in *Kirkham v Chief Constable of the Greater Manchester Police* [1990] 2 QB 283, 291:

> The *ex turpi causa* defence ultimately rests on a principle of public policy that the courts will not assist a plaintiff who has been guilty of illegal (or immoral) conduct of which the courts should take notice.

"illegal conduct" that was not also criminal being used *successfully* to invoke the operation of the illegality doctrine in a purely tort context. This one exception is *Hegarty v Shine*,[26] a case decided in 1878. The Court of Appeal in Ireland rejected a claim by a plaintiff for assault brought against the man she had been cohabiting with, but to whom she was not married. The plaintiff had contracted a venereal disease from the defendant, and claimed that the consent she had given to sexual intercourse had been vitiated by the defendant's deceit in concealing the fact that he had venereal disease. The Court held the relationship to be immoral[27] and refused to hear the claim.[28] However, we do not believe that this case would be decided in the same way today: such conduct would almost certainly not be regarded by a court as sufficiently immoral to impact on a claim for damages for physical injury.

1.15   There is one example of non-criminal behaviour that has featured (unsuccessfully) in recent years in the context of alleged illegality, and that is suicide. The cases of *Kirkham v Chief Constable of the Greater Manchester Police*[29] and *Reeves v Commissioner of Police of the Metropolis*[30] both arose out of the suicide of persons in police custody. In each case, the respective administratrix sued in negligence. In *Kirkham v Chief Constable of the Greater Manchester Police* it was argued by the defence that suicide, whilst no longer a crime, was still something that should bring into play the maxim *ex turpi causa non oritur actio*. The Court of Appeal rejected the application of this maxim, holding that such conduct would not "affront the public conscience" or "shock the ordinary citizen", at least where there is medical evidence that the suicide was not in full possession of his or her mind.[31] A similar defence was asserted in the later case of *Reeves v Commissioner of Police of the Metropolis*, it being argued that the Court of Appeal in *Kirkham* had

---

[26] (1877-82) 14 Cox CC 145.

[27] The judges were not shy in condemning the nature of the relationship, see the comments of Deasy LJA *ibid*, at p 152:

> In the present case the woman has led an immoral life - a life, one of the frequent consequences of which is the contraction of a loathsome disease...I am of opinion that such an investigation is no fit subject for the attention of a Court of Justice, and that no such investigation ought to receive judicial sanction.

[28] The basis of the decision seems to have been that the alleged fraud was by the man's concealment of his condition, and that such concealment would only be operative to vitiate the woman's consent if there was a duty between the parties to disclose capable of being enforced. See the comments of Palles CB *ibid*, at p 150:

> From such a relation, illegal and immoral in itself, no duty can arise, and in the absence of such duty, the concealment (although intentional and with a view to deceive), of a material fact, is in my opinion neither fraud nor evidence of fraud.

[29] [1990] 2 QB 283. See further below, para 2.37 n 89.

[30] [1999] QB 169. See further below, para 2.39 n 96.

[31] See further below, para 2.37 n 89. Lloyd LJ said at [1990] 2 QB 283, 291:

> [Suicide] is no longer regarded with the same abhorrence as it once was. It is, of course, impossible for us to say how far the change in public attitude has gone. But that there has been a change is beyond doubt.

We discuss the now-disapproved approach of assessing the "public conscience" below, paras 2.31-2.42.

left open the question of whether the suicide of a *sane* person would be sufficient for the illegality defence to apply. The Court of Appeal held that such action would not result in the successful application of the doctrine to bar the claim.[32]

1.16 We have found it difficult, although not impossible, to envisage a realistic modern day situation in which the conduct of the claimant is so immoral or reprehensible that the claim should be disallowed, without such conduct also being (potentially) criminal.[33] Nonetheless, we accept that such a case might occur, and references in this paper to illegality should be understood in the third, broadest sense noted above.

1.17 In the course of this paper we seek to avoid unnecessary use of Latin phrases such as *ex turpi causa non oritur actio*. Although honoured by tradition, we do not think that such phrases provide significant enlightenment to litigants in the twenty-first century, particularly given the attempts in recent years to make the process of civil litigation cheaper, clearer and fairer than before. Instead, although this may not be the ideal replacement, we refer in this paper to the "illegality doctrine" or the "defence of illegality".

4. AN OVERVIEW OF OUR PROVISIONAL PROPOSALS

1.18 Our provisional proposals for the reform of tort law are similar to those originally set out in Consultation Paper No 154 for contract and trusts, although we have since developed our thinking. We suggest that the current rules applied by the courts when considering the effect of illegality on a tortious claim should be replaced by a structured discretion, under which the court would be directed to

---

[32] See further below, para 2.39. Buxton LJ said at [1999] QB 169, 186:

> I am quite unpersuaded that shock or affront (both of which are very strong reactions indeed) would be the reaction of a citizen armed with that information [the circumstances of the case, and the respective responsibilities and duties] to an award of damages in respect of the suicide of a man known to be a suicide risk while he was involuntarily in police custody.

[33] *Clerk and Lindsell on Torts* (18th ed 2000) para 3-15 n 62 raises the question whether sado-masochistic practices not falling foul of the criminal law would fall into this category, and refers to the cases of *R v Brown* [1994] 1 AC 212 and *R v Wilson* [1997] QB 47. It seems that the House of Lords in the case of *R v Brown* thought there would be some such conduct that would be both morally repugnant yet legal. See, eg, the (dissenting) speech of Lord Mustill *ibid*, at p 257:

> The two remaining categories of conduct comprised private acts. Some were prosecuted and are now before the House. Others, which I have mentioned, were not. If repugnance to general public sentiments of morality and propriety were the test, one would have expected proceedings in respect of the most disgusting conduct to be prosecuted with the greater vigour. Yet the opposite is the case. Why is this so? Obviously because the prosecuting authorities could find no statutory prohibition apt to cover this conduct.

> However, whilst such conduct might come within a definition of "illegal", we are not at all sure that in most cases involving "grossly immoral" but consensual, non-criminal acts in private, denial of an allied civil claim for personal injury would be necessary to reflect the policies underlying the illegality doctrine. See below, Part IV.

consider whether, in the light of the underlying rationales and taking into account a number of guiding factors, the claim should be allowed or disallowed.

1.19   We propose that the discretion should be structured around a number of factors, to help provide certainty and guidance in the exercise of the discretion, and, importantly, to reflect the policies that lie behind the existence of the doctrine of illegality. In Consultation Paper No 154, and in the context of contract and trusts,[34] we proposed that those factors should be (i) the seriousness of the illegality; (ii) the knowledge and intention of the plaintiff[35] or illegal trust beneficiary; (iii) whether refusing to allow the claim or whether invalidity of the trust would act as a deterrent; (iv) whether refusing the claim would further the purpose of the rule which renders the contract or trust illegal, and (v) whether denying relief would be proportionate to the illegality involved. We discuss in Part VI the factors that we think are relevant to a discretion in the context of tort; they are along similar lines to those mentioned above. However, we will also raise other factors including one that reflects an argument that we discuss later in this paper, the need for "consistency".

5. OUR UNDERLYING THINKING

1.20   Our consideration of the law has led us to the conclusion that there are two problems with the current law. First, there is a lack of clarity in the way the illegality defence is to be applied in tort cases. Secondly, the law could be applied in a way which would produce outcomes that we think are undesirable, by including within its scope situations in which we believe the use of the illegality defence would be difficult to justify.

1.21   Our provisional proposals for reform do not seek to draw up a finite list of situations when illegality would impact on a claim and when it would not - this would be unjustifiably rigid and practically impossible - but we do seek to provide a policy-based, structured discretion to assist the court in deciding that question. Under these proposals, we envisage that cases where the claimant is seeking damages as compensation for the direct consequences of his or her illegal acts,[36] or seeking to be indemnified against such consequences, will generally continue to be barred by the courts.

1.22   However, there are several situations in which we feel that, although there is an element of illegality involved in the circumstances surrounding the claim, and *dicta* in recent cases that the defence may be available, barring the claim cannot reasonably be justified on the policy rationales that underlie the doctrine of illegality. In such cases we find it difficult to argue that the claimant should still be

---

[34]   Consultation Paper No 154, paras 7.43 and 8.63.

[35]   Now "claimant". In this paper we generally use the term "claimant" when referring hypothetically or to a case decided under the regime of the Civil Procedure Rules, and "plaintiff" when referring to a case decided before those Rules came into force.

[36]   Such as imprisonment (we think the High Court decision of *Meah v McCreamer* [1985] 1 All ER 367 to be wrong on this point - we develop this later in this paper. See below, paras 2.6 and 6.58).

denied what would be his or her 'normal' rights under the civil law. Barring a claim where it cannot be justified on grounds other than 'criminals shouldn't have rights' or on an unreasoned, 'gut-feeling' basis would be potentially disproportionate and wrong.

1.23 Although we can note at the outset of this paper that, with one exception, we do not regard any of the reported tort cases as being wrongly decided in terms of final *outcome*[37] - and to this extent our provisionally proposed reforms would not produce significantly different results - we do have significant concerns as to the current and potential future operation of the illegality doctrine. Many of the cases can be explained on a basis independent to that of illegality.[38] Despite the outcome, we do question the correctness of the decision on the illegality point in a number of cases. We find assistance in the approach taken by the Canadian Supreme Court, but we doubt whether some of the decisions in Australia should be followed in this country.[39]

1.24 As will be seen later in this paper, one of the possible consequences of our proposed reforms might be a reduction in the number of cases where the court relies on the illegality doctrine to bar claims for personal injuries. We recognise that some of the points we make in this paper may be controversial. Public opinion may not be in favour of any perceived increase in the ability of a criminal to sue for damages seemingly arising out of his or her criminal activity. This perception may be particularly acute where the tortfeasor is seen as the victim of the claimant's crime, such as the householder who uses excessive self-defence against the burglar, and who is then sued by that burglar for the injury caused.

1.25 However, we make the (perhaps) obvious point that the law does not allow even a criminal who has committed a serious offence to be deprived of all his or her rights under either the civil or criminal law. This would amount to outlawry, and this has quite clearly, and in our view rightly, been rejected by the courts.[40] Despite this, however, the law does recognise that in certain situations illegal conduct will as a matter of policy operate so as to prevent a person suing to enforce his or her rights under the civil law. The question is where the boundary is to be drawn between illegal conduct that will have an effect on the offender's rights, and where it will not. To be just, that boundary must not be drawn arbitrarily. It should

---

[37] The one exception is the case of *Meah v McCreamer, ibid.*

[38] A number of cases have featured not only illegality, but also defences such as self-defence, remoteness, *volenti non fit injuria* and lack of foreseeability to deny liability. See below, Part II for a detailed examination of the cases.

[39] See below, Part III for a discussion of comparative treatment of illegality in tort.

[40] See, eg, the comments of Judge LJ in *Cross v Kirkby, The Times* 5 April 2000:

> The medieval concept of outlawry is unacceptable in modern society. An outlaw forfeited the protection of the law. He could not invoke the assistance of the court to enforce non-existent rights. In the United Kingdom today there are no outlaws. However abhorrent the crime, whatever the subsequent conviction, the protection of the law extends to the criminal who enjoys rights not only in theory but enforceable in practice. (Smith Bernal transcript).

See further below, para 2.5.

reflect the underlying policy rationales. We believe that the outcomes of the existing cases can be justified in terms of the policy rationales or of other doctrines, but we are not convinced that this is true of the statements of law contained in some of the cases.

1.26 Finally, we make the point that the decision to bar a claimant from recovering damages in tort is a very serious one. It may mean that a claimant who has been barred from recovering damages for serious personal injury following a negligently caused accident will lose a substantial sum of money. He or she may have to fall back onto State benefits in respect of, for example, an inability to work as a result of the injury. In such a case this would involve both a substantial reduction in the sums available and a transfer of the financial responsibility from the defendant tortfeasor (or his or her insurers) to the public purse, the Criminal Injuries Compensation Authority, or possibly the Motor Insurers' Bureau. We consider these aspects in more detail in Parts II and V. Given these points, we have serious doubts as to the appropriateness of the illegality doctrine operating in the context of personal injury cases. This is a theme we develop during the course of this consultation paper.

PART II
THE EXISTING LAW IN ENGLAND AND WALES

1. INTRODUCTION

2.1 The Latin maxim *ex turpi causa non oritur actio*[1] has been held to mean that "no cause of action may be founded on an immoral or illegal act".[2] The maxim seems first to have been applied in contract cases and some commentators have argued that the maxim should not apply to tort claims.[3] Some of the earlier cases are unclear on this point,[4] but it has now been confirmed unequivocally that the defence does apply in tort,[5] and indeed the defence is said to be the same in both contract and tort. In *Standard Chartered Bank v Pakistan National Shipping Corporation and others (No 2)*[6] Aldous LJ said:

> There is in my view but one principle that is applicable to actions based upon contract, tort or recovery of property. It is, that public policy requires that the Courts will not lend their aid to a man who founds his action upon an immoral or illegal act.[7]

2.2 However, it remains difficult to identify when a claim in tort will be barred on the basis of the defence of illegality:[8] part of the difficulty stems from the wide variety of factual situations in which the illegal conduct may arise.

---

[1] Referred to below as *"ex turpi causa"*.

[2] *Revill v Newbery* [1996] QB 567, 576 *per* Neill LJ. See below, paras 2.49-2.52.

[3] See, eg, G Williams, "Contributory Negligence and Vicarious Liability" (1954) 17 MLR 365, 365 where he argued that "'plaintiff a wrongdoer' is not one of the general defences recognised in tort" although he acknowledged that Lord Asquith recognised a limited application of the defence in tort in *National Coal Board v England* [1954] AC 403. See below, para 2.48.

[4] In *National Coal Board v England*, *ibid*, at p 419 Lord Porter said:

> the adage itself is generally applied to a question of contract and I am by no means prepared to concede where concession is not required that it applies also to the case of a tort.

In the Australian case of *Smith v Jenkins* (1969) 119 CLR 397, 410 Windeyer J considered that *ex turpi causa* was not a valid defence in tort and that it should be understood as being confined to contract. See below, para 3.10.

[5] *Clunis v Camden and Islington Health Authority* [1998] QB 978, 987. See below, para 2.7.

[6] [2000] 1 Lloyd's Rep 218. See below, para 2.14 n 40.

[7] *Ibid*, at p 232. See also Mance LJ in *Hall v Woolston Hall Leisure Ltd* [2001] 1 WLR 225, 247:

> Although the underlying principle is as applicable to tort as it is to contract, its impact differs.

[8] Illegality is normally treated as a defence to a tort claim (see, eg, *Clerk and Lindsell on Torts* (18th ed 2000) paras 3-02 ff, and see the comments of Buxton LJ in *Reeves v Commissioner of Police of the Metropolis* [1999] QB 169, 186), even though it is clear that in contract, at least, the point may be raised by the court of its own motion: see Consultation Paper No 154, para

2. TYPES OF CASE

2.3   The cases in which claims in tort have been barred because some illegality was involved, or in which illegality was treated as a seriously arguable defence (even though it may ultimately have failed in the case), fall into several categories.

(1) Injury incurred in the course of an illegal joint venture

2.4   The best known category is perhaps where the claim is for compensation for injury suffered during the course of some illegal enterprise in which both the claimant and the defendant were involved. For example, in *Pitts v Hunt*[9] the plaintiff was a passenger on a motor cycle driven by the defendant. He was seriously injured when the motor cycle collided with another vehicle as a result of the defendant's negligent driving. The defendant was killed and the plaintiff brought an action for damages against the defendant's estate. Both had been drinking heavily prior to the accident and the plaintiff had encouraged the defendant to drive in a recklessly dangerous manner. The plaintiff was aware that the defendant was uninsured and did not hold a licence. The claim was dismissed on the basis that the plaintiff's own criminal conduct precluded him from recovering damages and the decision was upheld by the Court of Appeal.[10] There have been a number of other cases in which the plaintiff was seeking compensation for injuries suffered in the course of the illegal activity against a defendant who was participating with him in a joint illegal enterprise, for example *National Coal Board v England*,[11] *Murphy v Culhane*[12] and *Ashton v Turner*.[13]

6.5, and *Birkett v Acorn Business Machines Ltd* [1999] 2 All ER (Comm) 429. See also the comments of Megaw LJ in *Ferguson v Dawson and Partners* [1976] 1 WLR 1213, 1218:

> In the circumstances, although neither party has raised, nor wishes to raise, any issue as to the possible illegality...we thought it right to raise the question on our own initiative.

[9]   [1991] 1 QB 24.

[10]   See further below, paras 2.28-2.29. It was held that the defendant could not rely on a defence of willing acceptance of the risk (often referred to as *volenti non fit injuria*) because of the Road Traffic Act 1972, s 148(3). This provided that:

> if any other person is carried in or upon the vehicle while the user is so using it, any antecedent agreement or understanding between them (whether intended to be legally binding or not) shall be of no effect so far as it purports or might be held - (a) to negative or restrict any such liability of the user in respect of persons carried in or upon the vehicle as is required by section 203 of the Road Traffic Act 1960 to be covered by a policy of insurance; or (b) to impose any conditions with respect to the enforcement of any such liability of the user; and the fact that a person so carried has willingly accepted as his the risk of negligence on the part of the user shall not be treated as negativing any such liability of the user... .

This provision has been substantially reproduced in ss 149(2) and (3) of the Road Traffic Act 1988.

[11]   [1954] AC 403. See below, para 2.53.

[12]   [1977] QB 94. Cf *Lane v Holloway* [1968] 1 QB 379. See below, para 2.57 n 139.

[13]   [1981] 1 QB 137. See below, para 2.27.

(2) Injury in the course of the claimant's illegal activity

2.5 In other cases the defendant was 'innocent' of wrongdoing other than the alleged tort.[14] A recent example is *Cross v Kirkby*,[15] where the claimant, a hunt protester, attacked the defendant, a farmer, with a broken baseball bat. The defendant wrested the bat from him and in the struggle seriously injured the claimant, cracking his skull. The claimant's claim for compensation was dismissed by the Court of Appeal on the grounds that the defendant had acted in self defence and, had the action not failed on this ground, it would have failed because the claimant's injury arose out of his own unlawful acts. Another example is *Revill v Newbery*,[16] a much-publicised case in which an allotment holder shot and wounded a would-be burglar, although in this case the Court of Appeal held that the claim should not be barred on the ground of illegality.[17]

(3) Compensation for detention as a result of the claimant's crime

2.6 There have been several cases in which the plaintiff, having been convicted of a crime, sought compensation from the defendant tortfeasor in respect of imprisonment or other adverse consequences consequent upon that conviction, it being alleged that the crime would not have been committed but for the defendant's tort. A well known example is *Meah v McCreamer*.[18] The plaintiff suffered head injuries and brain damage as a result of the defendant's negligent driving, which led to a personality disorder. Four years later he sexually assaulted and raped three women. The illegality point was not raised and the plaintiff was held to be entitled to damages to compensate him for being imprisoned following his conviction. It is widely thought that, had the illegality point been argued, the claim would have been disallowed.[19]

2.7 In *Clunis v Camden and Islington Health Authority*[20] a similar type of claim was disallowed. The plaintiff had been discharged from hospital where he had been detained under section 3 of the Mental Health Act 1983, and was to receive after-care services in the community as provided for by section 117 of that Act. His mental condition deteriorated and two months later he stabbed a stranger to death at a London Underground station. He pleaded guilty to manslaughter on the grounds of diminished responsibility and was ordered to be detained in a

---

[14] There has been some suggestion in cases in Australia that the defence is confined to "illegal joint venture" cases, but it has been pointed out both there and in English cases that it would be illogical to allow the defence against a partner in crime but to refuse to apply it to an otherwise innocent tortfeasor. See, eg, the judgments of Schiemann and Beldam LJJ in *Sacco v Chief Constable of South Wales Constabulary* (unreported) 15 May 1998 (see below, paras 2.44-2.45).

[15] *The Times* 5 April 2000. We have also used a Smith Bernal transcript of this case.

[16] [1996] QB 567.

[17] See below, paras 2.49-2.52.

[18] [1985] 1 All ER 367.

[19] Beldam LJ cast doubt on the correctness of *Meah v McCreamer* in both *Clunis v Camden and Islington Health Authority* [1998] QB 978 and *Worrall v British Railways Board* (unreported) 29 April 1999.

[20] [1998] QB 978.

13

secure hospital. He subsequently brought an action against his local health authority for negligence. The health authority applied to strike out the claim as disclosing no cause of action on two grounds. First, that the claim arose out of the health authority's statutory obligations under section 117 of the 1983 Act and those obligations did not give rise to a common law duty of care. Secondly, that the claim was based on the plaintiff's own illegal act which amounted to manslaughter. In the Court of Appeal the health authority's appeal was allowed on both grounds.[21]

(4) Indemnity for liability arising from the claimant's crime

2.8 In some of the reported cases the plaintiff sought not compensation for his imprisonment but an indemnity for his liability to his victims or others. An example is *Meah v McCreamer and others (No. 2)*,[22] in which the plaintiff sought to be indemnified by the negligent driver and his insurers for the amounts he had been ordered to pay in compensation to his victims. The plaintiff's action was dismissed. Woolf J recorded that in *Meah v McCreamer*[23] it had not been argued for the defendant that the plaintiff was not entitled to be compensated for having committed the crimes, and so it was held that he was entitled to receive substantial damages in respect of that claim. This time it was argued that it would be contrary to public policy for the plaintiff to be indemnified in respect of the consequences of his crimes. Woolf J held that the action would be dismissed on two grounds. First, the damages were too remote to be recoverable. The plaintiff was not seeking damages for his own personal injuries or direct financial loss, but indirect loss for which the victims could not have sued the driver directly as no duty of care was owed to them. In addition, it would leave insurers open to indefinite liability for an indefinite duration. Secondly, it would be "distasteful" and contrary to public policy for the claimant to be indemnified in respect of the consequences of his crimes.[24]

(5) Compensation for the defendant's fraud or other wrongs

2.9 Several cases involve claims for compensation for fraud or other wrongs which took place in the context of an illegal transaction. For example, in *Saunders v Edwards*[25] the plaintiffs sued for fraudulent misrepresentation regarding the sale of

---

[21] See also *Askey v Golden Wine Co Ltd* [1948] 2 All ER 35, in which the issue was compensation for financial losses incurred by the plaintiff as a result of his criminal act (see further below, para 2.21). See also *Hardy v Motor Insurers' Bureau* [1964] 2 QB 745, where the plaintiff, a security guard who had been injured by a driver (who was subsequently convicted of inflicting grievous bodily harm), was able to recover compensation from the MIB. In this case, the illegality was the defendant's; the MIB sought to use this (unsuccessfully) to argue that they had no liability to satisfy the judgment. It was suggested *ibid,* at pp 760-761 and 769 that, although the plaintiff could recover, the defendant would have been barred had he sought an indemnity under a policy of insurance in respect of damages that he had already paid out in respect of his crime.

[22] [1986] 1 All ER 943. The case arose from the same facts as *Meah v McCreamer* [1985] 1 All ER 367. See above, para 2.6.

[23] *Ibid.*

[24] [1986] 1 All ER 943, 950.

[25] [1987] 1 WLR 1116.

a flat. The defendant had fraudulently represented that the lease of a flat included a roof garden. The plaintiffs had co-operated with the defendant in undervaluing the flat, and overstating the value of various chattels also sold, in order to avoid paying stamp duty. In the event the Court of Appeal allowed the claim to proceed as the plaintiffs' own fraud on the Inland Revenue was independent of, and unconnected to, the fraud of which the plaintiffs were victims. As it happens, the claims were also allowed in the other reported cases falling into this category, also because the illegality was not closely connected to the alleged wrong giving rise to the claim.[26] However, it seems that the claim would be disallowed were the connection close enough, for example, if to allow the claim would amount, in effect, to enforcing an illegal contract.[27]

(6) Conversion

2.10 Lastly, the claim may be for conversion of property which is the proceeds of fraud or other crime. In *Thackwell v Barclays Bank Ltd*[28] the plaintiff claimed for conversion of a cheque which represented the proceeds of fraud and his claim was disallowed on the basis that he was a knowing participant in the fraud. A more recent example is *Webb v Chief Constable of Merseyside Police*,[29] where the claimant successfully recovered from the police money which was alleged to be the proceeds of drug dealing.[30]

3. HOW CAN THE PRINCIPLES BE SUMMARISED?

2.11 As we have seen, the range of cases in which the defence of illegality has featured is wide. It is not easy to state the principles governing this defence in tort other than in broad terms. One possible analysis is that a claim in tort will fail on any of three grounds:

(1) where the claimant seeks, or is forced, to found the claim on his or her own illegal act;

(2) where the grant of relief to the claimant would enable him or her to benefit from his or her criminal conduct (or where what is sought is compensation for loss of liberty or an indemnity for the consequences of criminal behaviour); and

---

[26] See *Standard Chartered Bank v Pakistan National Shipping Corporation and others (No 2)* [2000] 1 Lloyd's Rep 218, discussed below, para 2.14 n 40, and *Hall v Woolston Hall Leisure Ltd* [2001] 1 WLR 225 (a sex discrimination case), discussed below, para 2.55.

[27] We said something similar in Consultation Paper No 154, where we suggested that a court would not award restitution where the award would have the same effect as the enforcement of a contract which the common law or statute refuses to enforce: see para 2.37 of that paper.

[28] [1986] 1 All ER 676. The case is well-known as the origin of the "public conscience" test subsequently disapproved by the House of Lords in *Tinsley v Milligan* [1994] 1 AC 340 (see below, paras 2.31-2.42) but this was not the actual ground of the decision.

[29] [2000] QB 427.

[30] See further below, para 2.14.

(3)   where, even though neither (1) nor (2) is applicable to the claim, the situation is nevertheless covered by a general residual principle that the court should not assist a claimant who has been guilty of illegal conduct of which the courts should take notice.[31]

2.12   This general residual principle, and possibly the other grounds, are subject to a number of limiting factors, relating to:

(a)   the statutory context,

(b)   the closeness of the causal link,

(c)   the seriousness of the illegality, and

(d)   the proportionality of the loss to the illegality.

We go on in this section to consider the grounds and the limiting factors in turn.

(1) The claimant cannot rely on an illegal act

2.13   This is sometimes referred to as "the *Bowmakers* principle"[32] or the rule in *Bowmakers Ltd v Barnet Instruments Ltd,*[33] although the case in fact involved the converse proposition that a claimant will be able to reclaim property if doing so does not involve reliance on the illegality. We discussed this case in Consultation Paper No 154.[34] The plaintiffs sued for conversion of machine-tools that the defendants had hired from the plaintiffs under hire purchase agreements which contravened statutory regulations. The Court of Appeal held the defendants liable for conversion in respect of the machine-tools. The plaintiffs did not seek to rely on the illegal contracts but rather they asserted that the machines were their property. The same principle was applied in *Tinsley v Milligan.*[35]

---

[31]   This is a similar analysis to that given by Kerr LJ in a contractual case, *Euro-Diam Ltd v Bathurst* [1990] 1 QB 1, 35. Kerr LJ rested his third category on the "public conscience" test. That test has since been discredited (see below, paras 2.31-2.42) but this does not mean that there is no third, 'general', category. See further below, paras 2.43-2.45.

[32]   See, eg, Staughton J at first instance in *Euro-Diam Ltd v Bathurst, ibid,* at p 18.

[33]   [1945] KB 65.

[34]   Consultation Paper No 154, paras 2.63-2.67.

[35]   [1994] 1 AC 340, where the House of Lords held that a claimant who can show good title without relying on the illegal act can recover property even if it was transferred or acquired for an illegal purpose. The broader view that a claimant without clean hands cannot enforce an equitable interest was rejected by the majority. For further discussion of the impact of this case, see below, paras 2.37-2.38. In *Euro-Diam Ltd v Bathurst* [1990] 1 QB 1, 35 Kerr LJ pointed out that where the claim does rest on the illegal act:

[f]or that purpose it makes no difference whether the illegality is raised in the plaintiff's claim or by way of reply to a ground of defence.

By way of example, he cited *Taylor v Chester* (1869) LR 4 QB 309, *Gascoigne v Gascoigne* [1918] 1 KB 223 and *In re Emery's Investment Trust* [1959] Ch 410.

16

2.14 Not surprisingly, the rule is referred to in cases in which the claim is for conversion of property. In *Webb v Chief Constable of Merseyside Police*[36] the Court of Appeal considered whether the police could refuse to return money to one of the claimants which they had lawfully seized from him, believing it to be the proceeds of drug-trafficking. This case differed from the usual situation where the contest to entitlement of the goods was between the claimant and the defendant as the police admitted they had no title to the money.[37] However, the Chief Constable sought to rely in civil proceedings on evidence that the money did come from drug trafficking. He argued that it would be absurd to lend assistance to the claimants which would enable them to complete their unlawful enterprise and that the court should not indirectly assist or encourage criminal acts. Applying *Tinsley v Milligan*,[38] and holding that it was irrelevant that illegality surrounding the claimant's acquisition of the money was pleaded in the defence or emerged in evidence, the Court of Appeal unanimously allowed that claimant's claim: he had established an entitlement to possession. In addition, the return to him of the money would not constitute completion of a crime.[39] The "no reliance" principle is also referred to in other situations, for example where there is a claim for a fraud committed in the context of a transaction involving some other illegality.[40]

2.15 The *Bowmakers* principle was applied to defeat a claim in the rather different context of *Clunis v Camden and Islington Health Authority*.[41] Beldam LJ, giving the judgment of the court, held that section 177 of the Mental Health Act 1983, which provided for the after-care services which the plaintiff should have received, was not apposite to create a cause of action in private law; but in addition, that the claim arose out of, and depended upon proof of, the plaintiff's commission of a criminal offence and that this would preclude the court from entertaining the

---

[36] [2000] QB 427.

[37] Although the money had been lawfully seized, the police's statutory powers to retain it had been exhausted.

[38] [1994] 1 AC 340.

[39] May LJ held that if he had committed a crime which resulted in his possession of the money, the crime was already complete before the police seized the money. See further below, para 2.41.

[40] In the recent case of *Standard Chartered Bank v Pakistan National Shipping Corporation and others (No 2)* [2000] 1 Lloyd's Rep 218 the defence was also advanced unsuccessfully. The claimant bank had been presented by charterers with a bill of lading which contained a false statement regarding the date of shipment. Other documents were presented out of time. The bill was accepted by the claimants and the charterers were paid. Later the claimants discovered the fraud, but nonetheless presented the documents to the issuing bank, falsely representing that they had been presented in time, in the hope that they would be accepted. The issuing bank rejected the documents and the claimants then brought an action for fraud against the carrier. The question for the Court of Appeal was whether the fact that the claimants had attempted to deceive a third party (the issuing bank) was a relevant factor in determining whether the defendants were liable to pay the full damages claimed in the tort of deceit. Evans LJ held that the conduct of the claimants was not so egregious, and the share of its responsibility for its own loss was not so weighty, that the court should refuse to entertain the claim. Aldous and Ward LJJ considered that the claimants' illegality was not relevant because they did not need to rely on their own illegality in order to found their claim.

[41] [1998] QB 978. See above, para 2.7.

claim unless it could be said that the plaintiff did not know the nature and quality of his act or that what he was doing was wrong.[42] *Clunis v Camden and Islington Health Authority* has also been followed in the recent case of *Worrall v British Railways Board*,[43] where the claimant sought damages in respect of imprisonment and lost earnings, alleged to have arisen out of his conviction for serious sexual offences.[44]

2.16 Thus it seems that a claim in tort will fail if, in order to make out the case, the claimant must rely on an illegal act. It might seem that, conversely, the claim will not fail if the claimant does not have to rely on the illegal act. However, this may not be the end of the enquiry.

2.17 First, in relation to claims for the conversion of property, there is an apparent exception for property which would be illegal for the claimant to possess. In *Bowmakers Ltd v Barnet Instruments Ltd*[45] du Parcq LJ stated that the general rule was not one of absolute application. One obvious exception was that class of cases where the goods claimed were unlawful to deal in at all: he gave the example of obscene books and speculated that there were others but thought it unnecessary to provide an exhaustive list.[46] In *Webb v Chief Constable of Merseyside Police*[47] the Chief Constable argued that possession of the money was an offence in itself and

---

[42] *Ibid*, at p 989. Had the plaintiff not known the nature and quality of his act or that what he was doing was wrong, he should have been found not guilty of the offence by reason of insanity. The knowledge or intention of the claimant seems to be an important factor. In *Worrall v British Railways Board* (unreported) 29 April 1999 (see below, n 44) Beldam LJ again noted that:

> In the present case the plaintiff did not argue at his trial in the Crown Court that he was not responsible in law for the offences he had committed.... Thus the commission of the offences was not excusable nor, it is to be noted, were psychiatric considerations put forward in mitigation of sentence. (Smith Bernal transcript).

Buxton LJ said in *Reeves v Commissioner of Police of the Metropolis* [1999] QB 169, 186 (see below, para 2.39):

> While it may be *more obviously objectionable, as the court in* [*Kirkham v Chief Constable of the Greater Manchester Police* [1990] 2 QB 283] *held, to hold an act by a mentally ill person to be morally repugnant*, the question for this court is whether that act should deprive him of relief in the law of negligence. (Emphasis added).

[43] (Unreported) 29 April 1999.

[44] A rail technician suffered an electric shock whilst working near a track, and claimed that this led to a personality disorder which led him to commit the sexual offences for which he was imprisoned. He sought to recover damages from his employers in respect of these offences and his inability to work. He claimed lost earnings and pension rights as a result of his dismissal (following his conviction). The defendants admitted negligence but the Court of Appeal held that the claim could not proceed because it arose *ex turpi causa*. Despite attempts by the claimant to distinguish *Clunis v Camden and Islington Health Authority* [1998] QB 978, Beldam LJ considered that the claimant's claim was "founded" on his crimes and so the case was held to be indistinguishable. Mummery LJ also considered that the claimant was pleading and relying on his own illegality.

[45] [1945] KB 65.

[46] [1945] KB 65, 72.

[47] [2000] QB 427, 444. See above, para 2.14.

therefore fell within the exception to the *Bowmakers* principle. The Court of Appeal held that the money claimed did not fall within the prohibited goods exception laid down in that case, but May LJ said that the claim might have failed had it been one for goods in which it was prohibited to deal, such as drugs.

2.18 Secondly, there may also be an exception where to order the return of property would enable the claimant to complete his or her crime.[48] Thirdly, the claim may also fail if it falls within the general category noted above.[49] This depends in part on the effect of the decision of the House of Lords in *Tinsley v Milligan*,[50] and is discussed below.[51]

(2) No benefit from an illegal act

2.19 The second ground is that the action is barred where the grant of relief to the claimant would enable him or her to benefit from his or her criminal conduct. This ground most often applies to defeat claims based on contract, as in the leading case of *Beresford v Royal Insurance Co Ltd*.[52] A life insurance policy condition provided that if the assured committed suicide within a year of taking out the policy it would be void. The assured committed suicide nine years after the policy was issued. The House of Lords held that even if it could be said that there was an implied undertaking by the insurance company to pay in the event of suicide occurring more than a year after the policy began, it would be contrary to public policy for either the person committing the crime or his representative to benefit from the crime.[53] Such a contract would therefore be unenforceable.[54]

2.20 A well-known application of the *Beresford* principle is *Gray and another v Barr (Prudential Assurance Co Ltd, third party)*.[55] In that case the plaintiffs were the dependants and the administrator of the estate of a man who had been killed by the defendant in circumstances which the Court of Appeal held amounted to

---

[48] In *Webb v Chief Constable of Merseyside Police* [2000] QB 427, 446 May LJ reserved his opinion "without enthusiasm" on whether such an exception, derived from *Thackwell v Barclays Bank Ltd* [1986] 1 All ER 676, may have survived *Tinsley v Milligan* [1994] 1 AC 340.

[49] See above, para 2.11(3).

[50] [1994] 1 AC 340.

[51] See below, paras 2.31-2.42.

[52] [1938] AC 586. See Consultation Paper No 154, paras 6.7-6.8.

[53] Suicide is no longer a crime. Cf above, para 1.15.

[54] See the comments of Lord Atkin, at [1938] AC 586, 598-599:

> I think that the principle is that a man is not to be allowed to have recourse to a Court of Justice to claim a benefit from his crime whether under a contract or a gift. No doubt the rule pays regard to the fact that to hold otherwise would in some cases offer an inducement to crime or remove a restraint to crime, and that its effect is to act as a deterrent to crime. But apart from these considerations the absolute rule is that the Courts will not recognize a benefit accruing to a criminal from his crime.

[55] [1971] 2 QB 554.

manslaughter.[56] The plaintiffs brought a claim in tort against the defendant, who claimed an indemnity from insurers under a policy which covered liability to third parties. The event was held to be outside the terms of the policy, but the court held also that it would be contrary to public policy to allow the claim against the insurer.

2.21 The *Beresford* principle was also applied in *Askey v Golden Wine Co Ltd*,[57] where the claim was for damages for fraud. As a result of the defendant's fraud the plaintiff adulterated drinks in breach of the Food and Drugs Act 1938, for which he was convicted and fined. Following the plaintiff's conviction all retailers with the offending liquor returned the bottles and were reimbursed by him. The plaintiff sought to recover damages for his loss of reputation, and an indemnity in respect of the fines and costs imposed as a result of his conviction, as well as in respect of the sums he had had to repay the retailers. His claim failed as it arose *ex turpi causa*. Denning J held that although he was not a party to the conspiracy to contaminate the drinks he was guilty of gross negligence. The plaintiff could not show that he had exercised all due diligence and that he had no reason to believe that the liquor was contaminated. For this reason Denning J held that the plaintiff could not recover the damages, fines or costs claimed:

> It is, I think, a principle of our law that the punishment inflicted by a criminal court is personal to the offender, and that the civil courts will not entertain an action by the offender to recover an indemnity against the consequences of that punishment. In every criminal court the punishment is fixed having regard to the personal responsibility of the offender in respect of the offence, to the necessity for deterring him and others from doing the same thing again, to reform him, and, in cases such as the present, to make him and others more careful in their dealings... . All these objects would be nullified if the offender could recover the amount of the fine and costs from another by process of the civil courts.[58]

He also held that the sums the plaintiff had to repay the retailers was reparation for his own crime of selling contaminated liquor without lawful excuse, and that public policy required that no right of indemnity, contribution or damages should be enforced in respect of expenses which the plaintiff had incurred by reason of being compelled to make reparation for his own crime.[59]

2.22 It will be recalled that in *Meah v McCreamer and others (No 2)*[60] that the plaintiff sought to be indemnified by the driver for the amounts he had been ordered to pay in compensation to his victims.[61] His action was dismissed. The second ground was the illegality of the plaintiff's conduct. Basing himself on the

[56] The defendant had in fact been acquitted of the criminal offence.

[57] [1948] 2 All ER 35.

[58] *Ibid*, at p 38.

[59] *Ibid*, at pp 38-39.

[60] [1986] 1 All ER 943. See above, para 2.8.

[61] See *W v Meah, D v Meah* [1986] 1 All ER 935.

judgment of Lord Denning MR in *Gray and another v Barr (Prudential Assurance Co Ltd, third party)*[62] Woolf J held that it would be "distasteful" and contrary to public policy for the claimant to be indemnified in respect of the consequences of his crimes.[63]

2.23 Thus there are clear examples of a version of the "no benefit" ground being applied in tort cases. It is not clear how far the ground goes. The tort cases are not strictly speaking cases of "benefit", at least in the sense that the claimant is seeking a profit he or she hoped to make from his or her illegal activity. They are cases in which what is sought is an indemnity for losses or liabilities he or she has incurred as a result of his or her acts. Once we move away from "benefits" to "indemnities", it is hard to know what the limits of the principle are. In a sense the claimant who seeks compensation for injuries incurred in the course of his or her illegal activity is seeking an indemnity from the consequences of that activity. Yet such claims are sometimes allowed, and as Evans LJ has said:

> [It] is one thing to deny to a plaintiff any fruits from his illegal conduct, but different and more far-reaching to deprive him even of compensation for injury which he suffers and which otherwise he is entitled to recover at law.[64]

2.24 The result seems to be that claims for compensation for injury suffered through the defendant's negligence but in the course of some illegal activity are not treated as falling under the "no benefit" (or rather, "no indemnity") ground. However, they may still be barred under the general principle that we discuss below.

2.25 Although we can point to examples of the "no reliance" and "no benefit" grounds being applied in tort cases, it is not always easy to be sure which ground is to be applied: *Clunis v Camden and Islington Health Authority*[65] appears to have been decided on the no-reliance test, but on the facts the "no indemnity" test seems equally apposite; and a claim may avoid either rule yet fail under the general principle.

(3) The general residual principle

(i) The general principle

2.26 Turning now to cases which do not fall within either of the more specific grounds discussed, but yet in which claims are said to fail because of illegality, we find a considerable variety of reasoning in the cases, and sometimes within a single case. Two particular issues merit discussion.

---

[62] [1971] 2 QB 554.

[63] [1986] 1 All ER 943, 950.

[64] *Revill v Newbery* [1996] QB 567, 579. See further below, paras 4.38-4.41.

[65] [1998] QB 978.

(a) Defence or no duty?

2.27 In *Ashton v Turner*[66] two drunken men committed a burglary. While trying to escape, the first defendant, driving the second defendant's car with his permission,[67] caused an accident severely injuring the plaintiff, who was a passenger in the car. His claims were dismissed. Ewbank J considered that as a matter of public policy the defendants owed him no duty of care. In certain circumstances the law might not recognise that a duty of care was owed by one participant in a crime to another in relation to an act done in the course of the commission of the crime. Ewbank J was strongly influenced by the approach taken by the Australian courts to this issue.[68] He held in the alternative that even if a duty of care was owed, the plaintiff had willingly accepted as his the risk of negligence and injury resulting from it.[69]

2.28 A rather similar analysis was adopted by Balcombe LJ in *Pitts v Hunt*.[70] He considered that where parties are engaged in a joint criminal enterprise it is impossible for the courts to determine the standard of care appropriate in the circumstances. In such a situation, therefore, it was impossible to tell whether the duty had been breached. This may be viewed as a 'one stage' approach to the treatment of the illegality so that the duty of care is itself negated.

2.29 However, neither of the other members of the court in this case took the same approach. Dillon LJ held that the action failed because the plaintiff's injuries arose directly *ex turpi causa*, as they were a direct result of the plaintiff's deliberate participation in criminal activity.[71] Beldam LJ considered the correct approach to be to consider the question of public policy in the light of the Road Traffic Acts. He concluded that an award to the plaintiff of compensation would be precluded on grounds of public policy.[72] (This involves a 'two-stage' approach, deciding first whether a duty of care would be owed in the absence of the illegality and then deciding whether the illegality operated to bar the claim.) He said that he would be reluctant to hold that the driver owed no duty of care even towards his passenger.[73]

---

[66] [1981] 1 QB 137.

[67] The second defendant was not at the scene of the burglary.

[68] See below, paras 3.2-3.27.

[69] This aspect must now be doubted, as in *Pitts v Hunt* [1991] 1 QB 24 the Court of Appeal held that this defence cannot apply to a passenger in a motor vehicle because of (what was then) Road Traffic Act 1972, s 148(3). See above, para 2.4 n 10.

[70] [1991] 1 QB 24. For the facts see above, para 2.4.

[71] *Ibid*, at p 60.

[72] *Ibid*, at pp 45-46.

[73] *Ibid*, at pp 46-47.

2.30 Although the 'no-duty' approach has found considerable support in Australia,[74] it has found little further judicial support in England and Wales, and has been subject to academic criticism.[75]

(b) "Public conscience"

2.31 We described in Consultation Paper No 154 the development of the public conscience test and its rejection by the House of Lords in *Tinsley v Milligan*.[76] Most of the cases in which this test was developed were tort cases, and it appears that, for tort cases, something of this test survives, although in modified form. We therefore think it necessary to re-examine briefly this test in the context of tort.

2.32 In *Thackwell v Barclays Bank Ltd*[77] Hutchison J based his decision on a concession that if the plaintiff knew that the scheme was fraudulent (as the judge held that he did) he could not recover. The judge also accepted a submission from counsel that the plaintiff would not necessarily recover, even if he was unaware of the fraud. The court should look at the quality of the illegality relied on by the defendant and answer two questions:

> First, whether there had been illegality of which the court should take notice and, second, whether in all the circumstances it would be an affront to the public conscience if by affording him the relief sought the court was seen to be indirectly assisting or encouraging the plaintiff in his criminal act.[78]

2.33 This "public conscience" test attracted some judicial support in subsequent tort cases. In *Saunders v Edwards*[79] Nicholls LJ accepted it as:

> summarising neatly and explicitly the essence of the task on which, in broad terms, the court is engaged when seeking to give effect to the requirements of public policy in this field. I would add, however, at

---

[74] See below, paras 3.2-3.27.

[75] See, eg, N Enonchong, *Illegal Transactions* (1998), pp 114-115, where a number of criticisms of the 'no duty' approach are advanced. Enonchong's criticisms (referring to some points made by McLachlin J in the Canadian case of *Hall v Hebert* [1993] 2 SCR 159, a case which we consider below, in Part III) include, amongst other things, the following points: (1) if illegality goes to the question of duty, it will cease to be a defence to be established by the defendant and instead the onus will shift to the claimant to show why the claim should not fail. This would be an inappropriate shifting in the case of a power which is said to be exceptional; (2) shifting the analysis to the duty of care does not provide any new insight into the basic question of when the claimant's case should be defeated because of his or her own illegality; and (3) the approach through the duty of care gives rise to unnecessary complexity and makes this area of law even more uncertain than it already is. See also the criticisms advanced in *Clerk and Lindsell on Torts* (18th ed 2000) para 3-05. See further below, paras 3.39 and 5.16-5.18.

[76] [1994] 1 AC 340. See Consultation Paper No 154, Part IV.

[77] [1986] 1 All ER 676. See above, para 2.10.

[78] *Ibid*, at p 687.

[79] [1987] 1 WLR 1116. See above, para 2.9.

the end of the formulation the words 'or encouraging others in similar criminal acts'.[80]

2.34 Nicholls LJ held that the claim for fraud made in *Saunders v Edwards* was not made to enforce the contract nor was it strictly based on the contract although the contract was a material part of the history.[81] He thought that there was illegality in this case of which the court should take notice, but that the court must weigh the extent to which in granting the plaintiffs relief the court might indirectly be encouraging these plaintiffs in their tax evasion, or indirectly encouraging others in other cases to proceed similarly when apportioning a purchase price, against permitting the fraudulent defendant to retain the money received from the plaintiffs as a direct result of the fraudulent misrepresentation. It was pertinent that the plaintiffs' loss flowing from the defendant's fraud would have been the same irrespective of the precise way in which the price was apportioned between the flat and the chattels.[82]

2.35 Kerr LJ (in the same case) may also have relied on a public policy test to some extent as well as the causal approach relied on by Bingham LJ.[83] He remarked that *Shelley v Paddock*[84] and *Thackwell v Barclays Bank Ltd*[85] showed that the conduct and relative moral culpability of the parties may be relevant in determining whether the *ex turpi causa* defence should be applied as a matter of public policy.[86]

---

[80] *Ibid*, at p 1132.

[81] *Ibid*, at p 1131.

[82] A similar conclusion was reached in *Shelley v Paddock* [1980] 1 QB 348. The plaintiff was defrauded by the defendants' false representation that they had the authority to sell a house in Spain. The plaintiff paid the defendants £9500 for the house. The payment contravened the Exchange Control Act 1947, although the plaintiff was unaware of this. In an action for damages for fraud the defendants argued that this illegality in the transaction precluded the plaintiff from recovering. Lord Denning MR thought that in the circumstances of the "pretty swindle" the principle stated by Lord Mansfield in *Holman v Johnson* (1775) 1 Cowp 341; 98 ER 1120 did not apply. He acknowledged that there had been some cases where a plaintiff had been unable to recover where he had been guilty of evading exchange control or similar regulations but they concerned cases where both parties were participating in the illegal act and there was nothing to choose between them. It is evident from the judgments that the Court of Appeal attempted to move away from the strict rules associated with illegality and instead weighed up the relative merits of both sides. Lord Denning held that the defendants were guilty of far graver wrongdoing than the plaintiff, see, *ibid* at p 357:

> It is better to allow Miss Shelley to recover here rather than to allow the Paddocks to remain in possession of their unlawful gains... . The Paddocks were guilty of a swindle. It is only fair and just that they should not be allowed to keep the benefit of their fraud. The judge was quite right in holding that the Paddocks are liable despite their plea of illegality.

[83] See below, para 2.54.

[84] [1980] 1 QB 348.

[85] [1986] 1 All ER 676.

[86] [1987] 1 WLR 1116, 1127.

2.36   The public conscience test was later re-stated by Kerr LJ in *Euro-Diam Ltd v Bathurst*:[87]

> The *ex turpi causa* defence ultimately rests on a principle of public policy that the courts will not assist a plaintiff who has been guilty of illegal (or immoral) conduct of which the courts should take notice. It applies if in all the circumstances it would be an affront to the public conscience to grant the plaintiff the relief which he seeks because the court would thereby appear to assist or encourage the plaintiff in his illegal conduct or to encourage others in similar acts... .[88]

2.37   As we noted in Consultation Paper No 154, the public conscience test was applied by the Court of Appeal in *Tinsley v Milligan*.[89] However in the House of Lords it was rejected by both the majority and the minority.[90] The defendant in possession proceedings claimed a beneficial interest in a house, the legal title to which was in the plaintiff's sole name. The plaintiff resisted the claim on the basis that she and the defendant had been defrauding the Department of Social Security, and that the arrangements with the property had been made with this illegal purpose in mind. A majority of the House of Lords held that, notwithstanding the illegality, the defendant was entitled to the interest which she claimed.

2.38   As to the public conscience test, Lord Goff, speaking for the minority, argued that the principle developed by counsel for the defence in *Thackwell v Barclays Bank Ltd*[91] for a limited purpose, had been allowed to expand both in its terms and in its range of application so that it operated as a broad qualifying principle which modified and transformed the long established principles. Furthermore, he considered that this had occurred without addressing fundamental questions on whether the development was consistent with earlier authorities, suitable or

---

[87]   [1990] 1 QB 1.

[88]   *Ibid*, at p 35. His was the only full judgment: the other two judges simply agreed with Kerr LJ.

[89]   [1992] Ch 310. See Consultation Paper No 154, para 4.3. It had also applied the test in the contract case of *Howard v Shirlstar Container Transport Ltd* [1990] 1 WLR 1292; and the test had been applied by Lloyd LJ in *Kirkham v Chief Constable of the Greater Manchester Police* [1990] 2 QB 283. In the latter case the plaintiff, the wife of the deceased, brought an action under the Fatal Accident Act 1976. She claimed that her husband, who committed suicide whilst being detained in police custody despite being a known suicide risk, had been owed a duty by the police to take reasonable steps to prevent him from committing suicide and that this had been breached when the police had failed to complete a police form for the prison authorities, notifying them of his status. The Court of Appeal found a duty was owed to the deceased and that it had been breached. The police had assumed responsibility to the deceased and on the balance of probabilities the deceased would have been prevented from taking his own life had the police not acted negligently. The defendants raised *ex turpi causa* but this was rejected. See also *Reeves v Commissioner of Police of the Metropolis* [1999] QB 169. See below n 96.

[90]   [1994] 1 AC 340. See also Dillon LJ's criticism of the public conscience test in *Pitts v Hunt* [1991] 1 QB 24, 56 in relation to a claim in tort. He said:

> I find a test that depends on what would or would not be an affront to the public conscience very difficult to apply.

[91]   [1986] 1 All ER 676.

desirable. He concluded that the application of the public conscience test in the instant case was not consistent with earlier authorities binding on the Court of Appeal. Lord Browne-Wilkinson, speaking for the majority, said that:

> the consequences of being a party to an illegal transaction cannot depend...on such an imponderable factor as the extent to which the public conscience would be affronted by recognising rights created by illegal transactions.[92]

2.39   Subsequent tort cases seem to have taken slightly different attitudes to the public conscience test. In *Reeves v Commissioner of Police of the Metropolis*[93] Buxton LJ considered that Kerr LJ's formulation in *Euro-Diam Ltd v Bathurst*[94] remained a valuable guide to the basis of the defence.[95] None of the members of the court thought the claim should fail for illegality.[96]

---

[92]   [1994] 1 AC 340, 369.

[93]   [1999] QB 169.

[94]   [1990] QB 1, 35.

[95]   Buxton LJ said at [1999] QB 169, 185:

> the actual application of Kerr LJ's exposition of *ex turpi causa* in the *Euro-Diam* case itself has been disapproved [by *Tinsley v Milligan*]. Nevertheless, the exposition in my view remains a valuable guide to the basis of the defence, and was accepted as such by Lloyd LJ in the *Kirkham* case [1990] 2 QB 283.

It should perhaps be noted that *Kirkham v Chief Constable of the Greater Manchester Police* was decided before the House of Lords decided *Tinsley v Milligan*, and that it was cited in argument before the House when hearing that case. See also Part IV of Consultation Paper No 154.

[96]   The facts were that a man who was a known suicide risk took his own life in police custody, and the joint administratrix sued the police. At trial the defences of *volenti non fit injuria* and *novus actus interveniens* were held to apply; given this, no conclusion was reached on whether illegality should prevent the claim. The Court of Appeal reversed that decision, stating that those defences could not be relied upon where the intervening act complained of was the very act which the defendant had a duty to prevent. On the illegality point, Buxton LJ put forward three reasons why the illegality defence should not apply. First, in this case the alleged turpitudinous act was the very thing that the defendants had a duty to try to prevent: it would be inconsistent to say that the public conscience would be shocked if the claimant were allowed to recover when the police already had a private law as well as a public law duty to take reasonable steps to prevent suicide. Secondly, granting relief would not assist or encourage others in the deceased's position or their representatives, and that there was no element of profit or windfall benefit. Thirdly, he saw no distinction between persons who were suffering from a defined mental illness and persons who were not, and thought that the public would not be shocked or affronted by either class of known suicide risk recovering damages for a period whilst in police custody. Morritt LJ thought that the act of the deceased amounted to a break in the chain of causation (dissenting on this point). However, on the issue of illegality, he said that although it remained criminal to aid and abet a suicide that could not affect the position of those who, like the administratrix, claimed solely under the person who committed suicide. He did not think it appropriate for a court to brand as contrary to public policy or offensive to the public conscience an act which Parliament had so recently legalised. Lord Bingham CJ also thought that permitting recovery in this case would not covertly connive at or countenance suicide, nor would the conscience of the ordinary citizen be affronted.

2.40 In contrast, in *Clunis v Camden and Islington Health Authority*[97] counsel for the plaintiff argued that the correct approach was to apply the affront to the public conscience test and that the illegality defence should not apply where the plaintiff's degree of responsibility was diminished by reason of mental disorder. This would be consistent with the reasoning in *Kirkham v Chief Constable of the Greater Manchester Police*,[98] where it was held that awarding damages following suicide would not affront the public conscience where medical evidence showed that the victim was "not in full possession of his mind".[99] The Court of Appeal in *Clunis v Camden and Islington Health Authority* held that the public conscience test had been rejected by the House of Lords as unsatisfactory.[100] It was considered that, in the instant case where the plaintiff had been convicted of a serious offence, public policy would:

> preclude the court from entertaining the plaintiff's claim unless it could be said that he did not know the nature and quality of his act or that what he was doing was wrong.[101]

In a more recent Court of Appeal case, *Cross v Kirkby*,[102] Beldam LJ repeated that the public conscience test is not applicable in tortious actions.

2.41 The rejection of the public conscience test by the House of Lords was also emphasised by May LJ in *Webb v Chief Constable of Merseyside Police*.[103] Counsel for the police argued that it would be absurd for the court to lend its assistance to the claimant to enable him to complete his criminal enterprise. He argued that *Thackwell v Barclays Bank Ltd*[104] was correctly decided on its facts and to that extent had survived *Tinsley v Milligan*.[105] May LJ held that the principle formulated by counsel in *Thackwell v Barclays Bank Ltd* and accepted by Hutchison J did not survive the decision of the House of Lords, though he would not rule out the possibility that circumstances might arise where the court could refuse relief if to grant it would be "indirectly assisting or encouraging the plaintiff in his criminal act." Presumably the gloss put on the principle by Nicholls LJ - "or encouraging others in similar criminal acts"[106] - survives also.

---

[97] [1998] QB 978. See above, para 2.7.

[98] [1990] 2 QB 283.

[99] *Ibid*, at p 291 *per* Lloyd LJ.

[100] [1998] QB 978, 989.

[101] *Ibid, per* Beldam LJ, giving the judgment of the court.

[102] *The Times* 5 April 2000. See above, para 2.5.

[103] [2000] QB 427. See above, para 2.14.

[104] [1986] 1 All ER 676.

[105] [1994] 1 AC 340.

[106] See above, para 2.33.

2.42 What seems not to survive is the notion of balancing the positions of the claimant and defendant. With one exception,[107] there has been no further reference to this in the cases since *Tinsley v Milligan*. Instead these have tended to refer back to Lord Mansfield's judgment in *Holman v Johnson* with its emphasis that the defence is:

> not for the sake of the defendant but because they [the courts] will not lend their aid to such a plaintiff.[108]

As Lord Goff explained in his dissenting speech in *Tinsley v Milligan*:

> the principle is not a principle of justice; it is a principle of policy, whose application is indiscriminate and so can lead to unfair consequences as between the parties to litigation.[109]

(ii) Application of the general principle

2.43 Whether or not any part of the *Thackwell* principle survives, there can be no doubt that a claim can be defeated by reason of illegality even where the claimant does not seek to benefit from the illegal act or to rely on the illegality in order to make out the claim. This general principle was applied most recently in *Cross v Kirkby*,[110] the case of the hunt protester injured by the person he was attacking.[111] The claimant unsuccessfully argued that illegality would only preclude his claim if he was forced to plead, give evidence of, or rely on his own illegality. Beldam LJ considered that such a technical approach was not present in Lord Mansfield's judgment in *Holman v Johnson*.[112] In his judgment, the correct question was whether:

> the claimant's claim is so closely connected or inextricably bound up with his own criminal or illegal conduct that the court could not permit him to recover without appearing to condone that conduct.[113]

Judge LJ reached the same conclusion.

2.44 The exact nature of this general principle is not always easy to discern. One recent example where the defence succeeded, but the basis upon which it did so is unclear, is *Sacco v Chief Constable of South Wales Constabulary*.[114] The plaintiff had been arrested and was placed in a police van. He attempted to escape from

---

[107] That one exception is the judgment of Evans LJ in *Standard Chartered Bank v Pakistan National Shipping Corporation and others (No 2)* [2000] 1 Lloyd's Rep 218, 230, but this was in the context of weighing the effect of competing causes. See below, para 2.61 n 152.

[108] (1775) 1 Cowp 341, 343; 98 ER 1120, 1121.

[109] [1994] 1 AC 340, 355.

[110] *The Times* 5 April 2000.

[111] See above, para 2.5.

[112] (1775) 1 Cowp 341; 98 ER 1120.

[113] Smith Bernal transcript.

[114] (Unreported) 15 May 1998.

custody by leaping out of the moving van, sustaining serious injuries. The Court of Appeal unanimously dismissed the appeal.[115] Schiemann LJ saw no reason to establish a new precedent to the effect that the police owe detainees a duty to prevent them harming themselves in the course of an escape, because by attempting to escape from lawful custody the plaintiff had been committing a crime.[116] In addition to this illegality point, he considered whether the plaintiff was the author of his own misfortune by doing something which he knew, or ought to have known, was dangerous, and thought that he was owed no duty by the police, his actions in kicking his way out of the van not being foreseeable.

2.45 Whilst Schiemann LJ was firm in the conclusion he reached, he was not as concerned with the mechanism used to refuse a remedy:

> Whether one expresses the refusal of a remedy as being based on absence of causation, absence of duty in these circumstances, absence of a breach of a wider duty, or as being based on the application of the principle that a plaintiff as a matter of policy is denied recovery in tort when his own wrongdoing is so much part of the claim that it cannot be overlooked, or because the plaintiff had voluntarily assumed the risk of injury, is perhaps a matter of jurisprudential predilection on the part of the judge.[117]

(iii) Limiting devices

2.46 While a residual general principle therefore continues to exist, it is also clear that, even if the "public conscience" test is no longer to be used, a claim for compensation will not always be barred merely because the claimant was involved in some illegal activity when he was injured.

2.47 In *Euro-Diam Ltd v Bathurst* Kerr LJ said that:

> the *ex turpi causa* defence must be approached pragmatically and with caution.[118]

---

[115] The plaintiff had sought a new trial on the basis of fresh evidence, and argued that the trial judge was wrong to hold that he was precluded from claiming damages for injury which arose out of his own criminal conduct in attempting to escape from lawful custody.

[116] He said:

> As a matter of legal policy I see no reason to permit a man to recover damages against the police if he hurts himself as part of that illegal enterprise. The basis of such recovery must be either an allegation of a breach of duty owed to him not to let him escape, or of a duty owed to him to take care that he does not hurt himself if he tries to escape. I see no reason to create such duties owed to him. It is common ground that the policy of the law is not to permit one criminal to recover damages from a fellow criminal who fails to take care of him whilst they are both engaged on a criminal enterprise. The reason for that rule is not the law's tenderness towards the criminal defendant, but the law's unwillingness to afford a criminal plaintiff a remedy in such circumstances. (Smith Bernal transcript).

[117] (Unreported) 15 May 1998 (Smith Bernal transcript).

[118] [1990] 1 QB 1, 35. See also Evans LJ in *Standard Chartered Bank v Pakistan National Shipping Corporation and others (No 2)* [2000] 1 Lloyd's Rep 218, 227:

A number of techniques for limiting the effect of the illegality doctrine have been used by the courts.

(a) The statutory context

2.48   In *National Coal Board v England*[119] the House of Lords ruled that a claim by the injured plaintiff should succeed notwithstanding the fact that he and a fellow employee, acting in concert, had knowingly broken regulations under the Coal Mines Act 1911 designed to protect workmen coupling up explosives. The House of Lords examined the legislative intention and found that the policy behind the statute did not preclude recovery in tort by the plaintiff.[120]

2.49   Equally, a statute may show that a claim is not to be defeated merely because the claimant was involved in some illegal activity when injured. In *Revill v Newbery*[121] the court concluded that awarding the plaintiff compensation for personal injuries did not constitute receiving a benefit from an illegal act, and his claim in negligence was upheld. The defendant was found liable because in discharging the

> the authorities support the 'pragmatic approach' described by Lord Justice Bingham in *Saunders v Edwards,* [1987] 1 WLR 1116 at p. 1134... .

See also the comments of Mance LJ in *Hall v Woolston Hall Leisure Ltd* [2001] 1 WLR 225, 248:

> in practice, as is evident, it requires quite extreme circumstances before the test will exclude a tort claim.

[119]   [1954] AC 403.

[120]   Such an approach has been adopted in a number of other cases. In *Cakebread v Hopping Brothers (Whetstone) Ltd* [1947] 1 KB 641 the plaintiff employee claimed for injuries suffered as a result of the employer's breach of the Woodworking Machinery Regulations 1922 and the Factories Act 1937. The employer raised the illegality defence, claiming that the plaintiff had aided and abetted the illegality. Even if that contention was correct, the defence failed because:

> [t]he policy of the Factories Act makes it plain that such a defence as that put forward here would be inconsistent with the intention of Parliament. (*per* Cohen LJ *ibid*, at p 654).

This can be contrasted with the case of *Hillen and another v ICI (Alkali) Ltd* [1934] 1 KB 455. Two stevedores breached the Docks Regulations 1925 by dangerously using the hatch coverings of the defendants' barge whilst loading a steamship. When the hatch coverings gave way the stevedores fell into the hold and were injured. In the Court of Appeal *ex turpi causa* operated to defeat their claim because the policy of those Regulations was to protect life and property, and persons who broke them knowingly should not be able to escape the effects of their conscious law-breaking. However, when the case went to the House of Lords it was not thought necessary to discuss the construction of the Regulations, and the case was decided on a ground which did not involve a finding of illegality. It was held that in acting as they did, the plaintiffs became trespassers, and, as such, the defendants owed no duty to them: see *Hillen and Pettigrew v ICI (Alkali) Ltd* [1936] AC 65, 69-70. See also *Pitts v Hunt* [1991] 1 QB 24, where Beldam LJ held that the public policy underlying the Road Traffic Acts demanded that the plaintiff's action be defeated by the defence.

[120]   [1954] AC 403, 428.

[121]   [1996] QB 567. See above, para 2.5.

shotgun in the direction of the burglar he had used greater violence than was justified by the use of reasonable force in lawful self-defence.[122]

2.50 Neill LJ founded his decision on the effect of the Occupier's Liability Act 1984.[123] He confined his consideration to the liability of someone in the position of the defendant towards an intruding burglar:

> It seems to me to be clear that, by enacting section 1 of the Act of 1984, Parliament has decided that an occupier cannot treat a burglar as an outlaw and has defined the scope of the duty owed to him. As I have already indicated, a person other than an occupier owes a similar duty to an intruder such as the plaintiff... . I am satisfied that the liability of someone in the position of the defendant is to be determined by applying a test similar to that set out in section 1(4) of the Act of 1984. There is in my view no room for a two-stage determination whereby the court considers first whether there has been a breach of duty and then considers whether notwithstanding a breach the plaintiff is barred from recovering by reason of the fact that he was engaged in crime.[124]

2.51 Evans LJ referred to the cases cited in Lord Goff's judgment in *Tinsley v Milligan*[125] and concluded that the cases of illegality in tort gave rise to different

---

[122] Prior to the 1984 Occupier's Liability Act judicial opinion indicated that a claim by a trespasser/criminal would fail because of the additional illegality. In *Cummings v Granger* [1977] QB 397, 406 Lord Denning said that:

> [a]ny thief or burglar who goes on to premises knowing that there is a guard-dog there ...[who] is bitten or injured...cannot recover. He voluntarily takes the risk of it. Even if he does not know there is a guard-dog there, he might be defeated by the plea '*ex turpi causa non oritur actio*'.

This view extended to personal injuries sustained by the plaintiff, even if he was shot. In *Murphy v Culhane* [1977] QB 94, 98 Lord Denning MR, with whose judgment Orr and Waller LJJ agreed, stated hypothetically that where a burglar was shot by a householder who used more force than was reasonably necessary, the householder may be guilty of manslaughter but he doubted whether the widow would have an action for damages as the householder might be able to use the defences of *ex turpi causa* or *volenti non fit injuria*.

[123] The relevant provisions of s 1 provide that:

> (3) An occupier of premises owes a duty to another (not being his visitor) in respect of any such risk as is referred to in subsection (1) above if - (a) he is aware of the danger or has reasonable grounds to believe that it exists; (b) he knows or has reasonable grounds to believe that the other is in the vicinity of the danger concerned or that he may come into the vicinity of the danger (in either case, whether the other has lawful authority for being in that vicinity or not); and (c) the risk is one against which, in all the circumstances of the case, he may reasonably be expected to offer the other some protection.

> (4) Where, by virtue of this section, an occupier of premises owes a duty to another in respect of such a risk, the duty is to take such care as is reasonable in all the circumstances of the case to see that he does not suffer injury on the premises by reason of the danger concerned.

[124] [1996] QB 567, 577.

[125] [1994] 1 AC 340.

considerations from those where an illegal transaction was involved.[126] In considering whether the maxim should operate to defeat the claim Evans LJ stated that the principle underlying the maxim was that the public interest required that the wrongdoer should not benefit from his crime or other offence. He was concerned that if it applied in the instant case then the trespasser who was also a criminal would be, effectively, an outlaw and debarred from recovering compensation for any injury he might sustain. He also made the point that to deny a person compensation for injury was different and more far-reaching than to refuse him the fruits of his illegal conduct.[127]

2.52   Millett LJ opined that the use of excessive force against an assailant or intruder was an actionable wrong and that there was no place for *ex turpi causa*. He did not consider it necessary to consider the joint criminal enterprise or application of *ex turpi causa* to other areas of tort, for:

> [i]f the doctrine applied, any claim by the assailant or trespasser would be barred no matter how excessive or unreasonable the force used against him.[128]

(b) A close connection

2.53   In *National Coal Board v England*[129] Lord Asquith said that if the loss or injury suffered is unrelated to the criminal act, *ex turpi causa* is not applicable. In his words, for *ex turpi causa* to apply the act must at least be a step in the execution of the common illegal purpose. He suggested that if two burglars, A and B, agree to open a safe using explosives and A so negligently handles the explosive charge as to injure B, B might find some difficulty in maintaining an action for negligence against A. On the other hand, if A and B are proceeding to the premises which they intend to burgle, and before they enter B picks A's pockets and steals his watch, he:

> [could not] believe that [he] could not sue in tort...[t]he theft is totally unconnected with the burglary.[130]

2.54   The clearest recent statement of the need to show a close link between the claimant's illegal act and the loss suffered is in the judgments of Kerr and Bingham LJJ in *Saunders v Edwards*.[131] Bingham LJ remarked that:

> Where issues of illegality are raised, the courts have...to steer a middle course between two unacceptable positions. On the one hand it is unacceptable that any court of law should aid or lend its authority to a party seeking to pursue or enforce an object or agreement which the

---

[126]   [1996] QB 567, 579.

[127]   See above, para 2.23.

[128]   [1996] QB 567, 580.

[129]   [1954] AC 403.

[130]   *Ibid*, at p 429.

[131]   [1987] 1 WLR 1116.

law prohibits. On the other hand, it is unacceptable that the court should, on the first indication of unlawfulness affecting any aspect of a transaction, draw up its skirts and refuse all assistance to the plaintiff, no matter how serious his loss nor how disproportionate his loss to the unlawfulness of his conduct.... . [O]n the whole the courts have tended to adopt a pragmatic approach to these problems, seeking where possible to see that genuine wrongs are righted so long as the court does not thereby promote or countenance a nefarious object or bargain which it is bound to condemn. Where the plaintiff's action in truth arises directly *ex turpi causa*, he is likely to fail...[w]here the plaintiff has suffered a genuine wrong, to which the allegedly unlawful conduct is incidental, he is likely to succeed... .[132]

Kerr LJ agreed that the plaintiffs' fraud on the Inland Revenue was independent of, and unconnected with, the fraud done to them. The plaintiffs' loss caused by the defendant's fraudulent misrepresentation would have been the same, even if the contract had not contained the illegal element. The plaintiffs' action was allowed to proceed.[133]

2.55 A further illustration of the need for a close connection between the illegal act and the claim is the case of *Hall v Woolston Hall Leisure Ltd*.[134] The claimant brought an action against her employer for sexual discrimination. The employer had failed to deduct income tax and National Insurance contributions from her wages. The Court of Appeal unanimously held that her acquiescence in this was not so closely connected with her claim that her claim should be barred.[135]

(c) Seriousness of the illegality

2.56 It is likely that even a claim which is inextricably linked to an illegal act will not fail unless the illegality is of a serious nature. In *Standard Chartered Bank v Pakistan National Shipping Corporation and others (No 2)*, Cresswell J said:

> Whatever theory founds a defence of *ex turpi*, the defendant must establish (a) that the plaintiff's conduct is so clearly reprehensible as to justify its condemnation by the Court and (b) that the conduct is so much part of the claim against the defendant...as to justify refusing any remedy to the plaintiff.[136]

---

[132] *Ibid*, at p 1134.

[133] *Ibid*, at p 1127. It will be recalled that Nicholls LJ reached the same conclusion as Kerr and Bingham LJJ although he took a slightly different approach, applying the public policy test derived from *Thackwell v Barclays Bank Ltd* [1986] 1 All ER 676. See above, paras 2.33-2.34.

[134] [2001] 1 WLR 225.

[135] See also the comments of Judge LJ in *Cross v Kirkby*, *The Times* 5 April 2000:

> In my judgment, where the claimant is behaving unlawfully, or criminally, on the occasion when his cause of action in tort arises, his claim is not liable to be defeated *ex turpi causa* unless it is also established that the facts which give rise to it are inextricably linked with his criminal conduct. (Smith Bernal transcript).

[136] [1998] 1 Lloyd's Rep 684, 705-706.

In the Court of Appeal Evans LJ said the judge had summarised the law "impeccably".[137]

2.57 In *Cross v Kirkby*[138] Beldam LJ sought to draw a distinction between the instant case and *Lane v Holloway*.[139] He considered *Lane v Holloway* as an example in which the claimant's illegality was to be regarded as trivial and not a cause of the assault for which he was claiming damages, and that therefore it was not appropriate to apply the doctrine. By contrast he viewed *Murphy v Culhane*[140] as an example of the Court of Appeal refusing to overlook criminal conduct which was serious and sufficiently connected with the act of the defendant. He held that *Cross v Kirkby* fell into the latter category.

2.58 This relevance of the seriousness of the illegality is a difficult area which has led one author to comment that:

> [i]t is not possible to state with any confidence how reprehensible the claimant's conduct must be...the more serious the offence the more likely it is that the defence will apply, though this is not automatically the case because of the "proportionality" requirement - the seriousness of the defendant's conduct may outweigh that of the claimant.[141]

However, such a principle may provide an explanation of cases such as *Revill v Newbery*.[142] The existence of the Occupier's Liability Act 1984 shows that not every trespass will be sufficient for *ex turpi causa* to operate; even a trespass with intent to burgle is not sufficiently serious to justify excluding a claim. This seems a better explanation of the distinction between this case and *Cross v Kirkby*[143] than to say that in the latter the claim was inextricably linked to the illegality whereas the shooting of the burglar was not.[144]

(d) Proportionality of loss to illegality

2.59 It is important to define carefully what is meant by this concept. It will be recalled that in *Saunders v Edwards*[145] Bingham LJ said that the court should not refuse all assistance to the plaintiff, no matter how serious the loss nor how disproportionate the loss to the unlawfulness of the conduct. The possible

---

[137] [2000] 1 Lloyd's Rep 218, 227.

[138] *The Times* 5 April 2000. See above, para 2.5.

[139] [1968] 1 QB 379. In this case the elderly plaintiff aimed a punch at the defendant because he thought he himself might be struck, and the Court of Appeal rejected the argument that no action lay because it was an unlawful fight.

[140] [1977] QB 94.

[141] *Clerk and Lindsell on Torts* (18th ed 2000) para 3-13.

[142] [1996] QB 567.

[143] *The Times* 5 April 2000.

[144] See the judgment of Judge LJ in *Cross v Kirkby, The Times* 5 April 2000.

[145] [1987] 1 WLR 1116.

"disproportion" referred to is between the claimant's conduct and the seriousness of the loss he or she will incur if his or her claim is disallowed.

2.60 The "public conscience test", particularly as developed and applied by Nicholls LJ in *Saunders v Edwards*[146] and *Tinsley v Milligan*,[147] involved proportionality in a different sense, that of balancing the actions of the defendant and claimant. We have already suggested that this does not seem to have survived the decision of the House of Lords in *Tinsley v Milligan*.[148]

2.61 Thus in *Cross v Kirkby*,[149] Beldam LJ was keen to point out the limitations of using proportionality as a factor in deciding whether *ex turpi causa* operated. He referred to the judgment below and stated that:

> the cases referred to by the judge do not lead to his conclusion that it is permissible in every case for the court to weigh up nicely the degree of illegality by the claimant on the one hand and the defendant on the other to decide which of them should be allowed to recover damages for an assault.[150]

Instead, he considered that when the judge referred to the proportionality of each party's behaviour towards the other in the context of assaults, the cases to which he referred were not based on a simple comparison between the force used by the parties. Rather the question was whether one of the parties whose illegal conduct might be regarded as trivial should be precluded from recovering damages if the retaliation had taken the form of an aggravated assault.[151] In other words, proportionality in the second sense, as between claimant and defendant, is relevant to questions of causation.[152] As we noted above, Beldam LJ concluded that *Lane v Holloway*[153] was a case where the plaintiff's illegality was sufficiently trivial and lacking in a causal link to be disregarded by the court.[154]

---

[146] *Ibid.*

[147] [1994] 1 AC 340.

[148] See above, para 2.42.

[149] *The Times* 5 April 2000.

[150] Smith Bernal transcript.

[151] In *Lane v Holloway* [1968] 1 QB 379 Lord Denning had argued that the defence did not operate because even if the fight started by being unlawful, the plaintiff was entitled to sue where the subsequent injury was inflicted by a weapon or a savage blow out of all proportion to the occasion.

[152] See also *Standard Chartered Bank v Pakistan National Shipping Corporation and others (No 2)* [2000] 1 Lloyd's Rep 218, in which Evans LJ held that it was necessary to decide whether the cause of the loss for which the claim was made was (1) the false statement in the bill of lading or (2) its decision to accept the documents late and pass them on to the issuing bank with a false statement as to when they had been presented. He said that in answering this the relative turpitude of the claimants' and the defendants' conduct had to be taken into account.

[153] [1968] 1 QB 379.

[154] See above, para 2.57.

(iv) Application of the limiting factors

2.62 The limiting factors also seem to apply *mutatis mutandis* to claims which might otherwise be based on the reliance on an illegal act or the no benefit grounds.[155]

(v) Non-condonation

2.63 There is an additional aspect of the general test in relation to the illegality defence that has been referred to in a number of cases. This is whether allowing the claim would give the impression that the court was condoning the claimant's illegal conduct, or whether it would encourage others. Hutchison J in *Thackwell v Barclays Bank Ltd*[156] said that he accepted the argument advanced by counsel for the defendants that the defence was allowed where finding for the plaintiff would be indirectly assisting or encouraging the plaintiff in his criminal, fraudulent or illegal activity.[157] Nicholls LJ referred to these comments in *Saunders v Edwards*,[158] holding the test to be a "useful and valuable one", and noting that he would add the words "or encouraging others in similar criminal acts".[159] We saw earlier that Kerr LJ in *Euro-Diam Ltd v Bathurst*[160] also referred to this test.[161]

2.64 At this stage, this aspect of assisting or encouraging the plaintiff appears to have formed part of the public conscience test. As we have seen, this test was rejected by the House of Lords in *Tinsley v Milligan*.[162] However, references to not condoning the conduct or not encouraging others continue in the tort cases even after this decision. In *Reeves v Commissioner of Police of the Metropolis*[163] the illegality defence was advanced unsuccessfully. Buxton LJ referred to Kerr LJ's comments in *Euro-Diam Ltd v Bathurst*[164] and noted that:

> To grant relief in our case *does not assist or encourage either [the deceased] or others* in his situation to continue in their disapproved conduct: and even less is that the effect of the grant of relief to [the deceased's] representatives. *Nor even are others in [the deceased's] position encouraged* to act on their representatives' behalf... .[165]

---

[155] See the words of Cresswell J at first instance in *Standard Chartered Bank v Pakistan National Shipping Corporation and others (No 2)* (a "reliance" case) quoted above, para 2.56.

[156] [1986] 1 All ER 676.

[157] *Ibid*, at p 689.

[158] [1987] 1 WLR 1116.

[159] *Ibid*, at p 1132.

[160] [1990] 1 QB 1.

[161] See above, para 2.36.

[162] [1994] 1 AC 340.

[163] [1999] QB 169. See above, para 2.39.

[164] [1990] 1 QB 1.

[165] [1999] QB 169, 185 (emphasis added).

2.65 Condonation again appeared in the judgment of Beldam LJ in *Cross v Kirkby*.[166] After expressly noting that the majority in *Tinsley v Milligan* had regarded the public conscience test as unsatisfactory, Beldam LJ went on to consider the test to be applied and concluded:

> In my view the principle applies when the claimant's claim is so closely connected or inextricably bound up with his own criminal or illegal conduct that the court could not permit him to recover *without appearing to condone that conduct.*[167]

2.66 This passage was cited by Peter Gibson LJ in the case of *Hall v Woolston Hall Leisure Ltd*[168] to support his view that:

> It therefore follows that the correct approach of the tribunal in a sex discrimination case should be to consider whether the applicant's claim arises out of or is so clearly connected to or inextricably bound up or linked with the illegal conduct of the applicant that the court could not permit the applicant to recover compensation *without appearing to condone that conduct.*[169]

2.67 It therefore seems that an important aspect of the test to be applied involves consideration of whether allowing the claim would appear either to condone the illegal conduct, or to encourage the claimant or others. This factor appears to have survived the rejection of the public conscience test and indeed appears to be the rationale currently given for the residual general principle. It is a point we return to later in this paper.[170]

4. OTHER SOURCES OF COMPENSATION

2.68 We stated in Part I that the decision to bar a claimant from recovering damages from the tortfeasor who may have caused him or her serious personal injury was a serious step. We noted that the effect of such a decision might in some cases be to throw the claimant back to looking for other sources of financial compensation in respect of those injuries. One such source would be the State, by way of benefit payments to a claimant who is unable to work by reason of his or her injuries. In such a case, the expense is borne by the State, not the individual tortfeasor or insurer.

2.69 There are two other schemes from which an injured party may obtain some compensation, rather than from the person responsible, although their operation in respect of a claimant who has acted illegally may be doubted. One is that operated by the Criminal Injuries Compensation Authority (CICA). In brief, this scheme allows for compensation awards to be made to victims of crimes of

---

[166] *The Times* 5 April 2000.

[167] Smith Bernal transcript (emphasis added).

[168] [2001] 1 WLR 225.

[169] *Ibid*, at p 237 (emphasis added).

[170] See below, paras 4.48-4.54.

violence. What is the relationship between this scheme and the illegality defence? We can envisage circumstances where the claimant has acted illegally, yet also been a victim of violence. Take, for example, the claimant in *Cross v Kirkby*.[171] In this case, the defendant was held to have been acting in self-defence. In addition, the Court held that even if the force had been excessive, the illegality defence would bar the claim. If we imagine that excessive force had been used by the defendant, then the claimant would have been the victim of a crime, but his own civil claim might have been barred because of his own illegal conduct. If this were the case, would such a claimant have recourse to the CICA if his civil claim were disallowed?

2.70 Some claimants might find that their illegal conduct prevents a claim to the CICA as well as a civil claim against the defendant. The 1996 Criminal Injuries Compensation Scheme[172] provides that an award can be reduced or withheld on account of the applicant's conduct before, during or after the incident,[173] or the applicant's character as shown by his or her criminal convictions.[174] In relation to "conduct", the guide to the Scheme issued by the CICA explains that:

> 'conduct' means something which can fairly be described as bad conduct or misconduct and includes provocative behaviour and offensive language.[175]

In relation to the "character" provisions, it notes:

> this is because a person who has committed criminal offences has probably caused distress and loss and injury to other persons, and has certainly caused considerable expense to society by reason of court appearances and the cost of supervising sentences, even when they have been non-custodial, and the victims may themselves have sought compensation, which is another charge on society. Even though an applicant may be blameless in the incident in which the injury was sustained, Parliament has nevertheless provided in the Scheme that convictions which are not spent under the Rehabilitation of Offenders Act 1974 should be taken into account.[176]

It seems *a fortiori* that a person who was involved in criminality at the time of his or her accident would be barred from recovering.[177]

---

[171] *The Times* 5 April 2000. See above, para 2.5.

[172] Set up under the Criminal Injuries Compensation Act 1995.

[173] Para 13 (d).

[174] Para 13 (e). For examples (under previous schemes) where awards have been denied or reduced because of the applicant's convictions, see *R v Criminal Injuries Compensation Board, ex p Thomas* [1995] PIQR P99, and *R v Criminal Injuries Compensation Board, ex p Moore, The Times* 14 May 1999.

[175] Para 8.14.

[176] Para 8.15.

[177] For further detail on the CICA Scheme, see, eg, D Miers, *State Compensation for Criminal Injuries* (1997) paras 7.5 ff.

2.71   The second scheme that might be relevant in the context of the illegality defence is that operated by the Motor Insurers' Bureau. This provides compensation to the victims of uninsured motorists in certain circumstances. Would an injured passenger whose civil claim against the driver had been barred for illegality be able to apply to the MIB for compensation? We think this unlikely. The rules of the schemes operating both in respect of uninsured drivers and untraced drivers exclude most of the circumstances in which the illegally acting claimant would find himself or herself. If the passenger knew, or ought to have known, that the vehicle had no insurance, or that it was being used in the furtherance of crime or as a means of escape from lawful apprehension, then no claim against the MIB can be made: this may mean there is no insurance at all.[178] So again, it would seem, a claimant who is denied relief against a tortfeasor in the civil courts is unlikely to receive compensation under this alternative scheme.

5. CONCLUSIONS

2.72   We started our consideration of the current law by noting that it was not easy to state the principles governing this defence other than in broad terms, and we suggested a possible analysis whereby a claim will fail on any of three grounds.[179] It is easy to agree with the comment of Buxton LJ in *Reeves v Commissioner of Police of the Metropolis* on the illegality defence:

> [t]he limits of this defence are very difficult to state or rationalise.[180]

However, we think that an analysis of the cases shows that a number of propositions can be made:

(1)   The illegality defence may apply to a claim[181] in tort if:

---

[178]   For a recent example in which the relevant rules of the MIB were considered by the House of Lords, see *White v White and another* [2001] 1 WLR 481. In the context of these rules, note the express reference to proportionality by Lord Nicholls *ibid*, at p 486:

> Proportionality requires that a high degree of personal fault must exist before it would be right for an injured passenger to be deprived of compensation.

[179]   See above, para 2.11.

[180]   [1999] QB 169, 184.

[181]   The illegality defence may operate to affect a head of damage, rather than the entire claim. See the comments of Mance LJ in *Hall v Woolston Hall Leisure Ltd* [2001] 1 WLR 225, 241:

> But I do not doubt that English Law recognises situations in which a claimant will be barred on grounds of illegality from pursuing a particular head of relief, rather than the whole of his or her claim.

It may also operate where the claim involves not an unlawful act in the past, but a situation where the claimant alleges a lost opportunity, if that would have necessarily involved the commission of an unlawful act. See *Rance v Mid-Downs Health Authority* [1991] 1 QB 587, where the plaintiff parents sued the health authority for negligently failing to diagnose their unborn child's severe handicap on the grounds that, but for their negligence, when the foetus was of about 26 weeks, the mother would have aborted the child. Brooke J held (as an alternative ground to finding that the defendants were not negligent) that the plaintiffs could not sue for their lost opportunity as at the material time such an abortion would have been illegal because of s 1 Infant Life (Preservation) Act 1929. He held that it was the duty of the

(a) the claimant must rely directly upon his or her own illegal act to found the case;

(b) the claimant is seeking to benefit from his or her own wrongdoing, or is seeking compensation for loss of liberty, or an indemnity for a fine or liability to third parties incurred, as the result of his or her criminal behaviour; or

(c) the claim falls within the residual general principle that the courts will not assist a claimant who has been guilty of illegal conduct if the court would thereby appear to condone such conduct, to assist or encourage the claimant in his or her illegal conduct or to encourage others in similar acts.

(2) It appears that the residual principle is limited by a number of factors, including at least:

(a) the purpose of the legislation;

(b) the closeness of connection of the illegal act to the claim;

(c) the seriousness of the illegality involved, and

(d) the proportionality between the claimant's conduct and the loss he or she will suffer if the claim is barred.

It may well be that principles (1)(a) and 1(b) are similarly limited.

2.73 In several cases where illegality has been raised as a defence it has not been successful. Examples are: *Revill v Newbery,*[182] *Hardy v Motor Insurers' Bureau,*[183] *Standard Chartered Bank v Pakistan National Shipping Corporation and others (No 2),*[184] and *Webb v Chief Constable of Merseyside Police.*[185] In a number of cases it has

court to deny the plaintiffs relief on public policy grounds once it was satisfied that the plaintiffs could only have turned their lost opportunity to value by terminating the life of a child who, on the balance of probabilities, was capable of being born alive.

See also *Briody formerly Moore v St Helen's and Knowsley Health Authority* [2000] 2 FCR 13, where it was held that it would be against public policy for the claimant to be awarded damages representing the cost of entering into a commercial surrogacy agreement when such agreements were unlawful and unenforceable under English law and when the chances of the process being successful in this case were very unlikely. Ebsworth J held (*ibid*, at pp 35-36):

[o]n any view of our law the claimant seeks an award of damages to acquire a child by methods which do not comply with that law.... It is one thing for a court retrospectively to sanction breaches of statute in the paramount interests of an existing child, it is quite another to award damages to enable such an unenforceable and unlawful contract to be entered into.

[182] [1996] QB 567. See above, paras 2.49-2.52.

[183] [1964] 2 QB 745. See above, para 2.7 n 21.

[184] [2000] 1 Lloyd's Rep 218. See above, para 2.14 n 40.

[185] [2000] QB 427. See above, para 2.14.

been applied but only as an alternative ground, as in: *Meah v McCreamer and others (No 2)*,[186] *Clunis v Camden and Islington Health Authority*,[187] *Sacco v Chief Constable of South Wales Constabulary*,[188] and *Cross v Kirkby*.[189] On occasions the defence has succeeded where another ground could have applied. For example, in *Pitts v Hunt*[190] the plaintiff's action might have been held to fail on the basis of an absence of a duty of care.[191] The same is true for *Ashton v Turner*.[192] In addition, were it not for the Road Traffic Acts, *volenti non fit injuria* would have explained the case. There have been cases in which the defence has succeeded when the claimant could only make the claim by relying on the illegal act (*Clunis v Camden and Islington Health Authority*[193]), or in which the claim was for compensation for loss of liberty (*Worrall v British Railways Board*[194]), or an indemnity for a fine (*Askey v Golden Wine Co Ltd*[195]) or liability to third parties incurred (*Meah v McCreamer and others (No 2)*[196]) as the result of his criminal behaviour. The only recent case where the illegality defence has operated as the sole ground to bar the claim appears to be *Worrall v British Railways Board*.[197]

---

[186] [1986] 1 All ER 943. See above, para 2.8.

[187] [1998] QB 978. See above, para 2.7.

[188] (Unreported) 15 May 1998. See above, paras 2.44-2.45.

[189] *The Times* 5 April 2000. See above, para 2.5.

[190] [1991] 1 QB 24. See above, paras 2.28-2.29.

[191] This was indeed the basis of Balcombe LJ's decision. See above, para 2.28.

[192] [1981] 1 QB 137. See above, para 2.27.

[193] [1998] QB 978.

[194] (Unreported) 29 April 1999. See above, para 2.15 n 44.

[195] [1948] 2 All ER 35. See above, para 2.21.

[196] [1986] 1 All ER 943.

[197] (Unreported) 29 April 1999.

PART III
COMPARATIVE LAW

3.1   In deciding on the form and details of our proposals, we have found it helpful to consider the law in a number of other countries, in particular Canada, Australia and New Zealand. The positions taken by these legal systems differ significantly from the position in English law and from each other. As we noted in Part II, the English courts have been influenced by developments in these countries, where the superior courts have had more opportunities to deal with the issue of illegality than their English counterparts. In this Part, we examine some of the issues which have arisen in these systems.

1. AUSTRALIA

(1) Is *ex turpi causa* recognised in tort?

3.2   The concept of a general defence of *ex turpi causa* in tort is not recognised as such in Australia. Nonetheless, a claim may be precluded on the basis that no duty is owed by the defendant to the plaintiff because the claim involves some form of illegality. A debate about the application and appropriateness of this approach - particularly as concerning cases of joint illegality - has dominated the cases in the High Court of Australia.

(2) In what situations will illegality prevent the duty of care from arising?

3.3   *Henwood v The Municipal Tramways Trust (SA)*[1] was the first case in which the High Court considered the effect of the plaintiff's illegality on an action in negligence. In breach of a by-law made by the tramway authority as a safety measure, a tram passenger leaned over a side rail on a tram in order to be sick. He was killed when his head struck two steel standards in the road. The High Court unanimously rejected the argument that no action in negligence lay because of that breach. Latham CJ concluded that there was no general principle of English law that a person who was engaged in some unlawful act was disabled from complaining of injury done to him by others. The extent of the duty of care was determined by the circumstances of the case which create that duty. A person injured in a car accident might be a child truanting from school or a burglar on his way to a job but in neither situation would the illegality be relevant for the purpose of deciding the existence, or defining the content, of the driver's duty not to injure them.[2]

3.4   Dixon and McTiernan JJ, in a combined judgment, stated that the important issue was the intention of the statute penalising the conduct:

> [I]n every case the question must be whether it is part of the purpose of the law against which the plaintiff has offended to disentitle a

---

[1]   (1938) 60 CLR 438.

[2]   *Ibid*, at p 446.

42

person doing the prohibited act from complaining of the other party's neglect or default, without which his own act would not have resulted in injury.[3]

3.5 They held that there was no rule denying to a person who was doing an unlawful thing the protection of the general law imposing upon others duties of care for that person's safety.[4] The general principle was that, in the absence of statutory intention to the effect that a person breaching a penal provision should be deprived of a private right of action, such a person would not be barred from bringing a claim.[5] Starke J had also considered that each case must rest upon the particular statute or by-law and the language employed.[6] The case was remitted to the trial judge to make findings of fact on the question of negligence and contributory negligence.

3.6 In contrast, in *Godbolt v Fittock*[7] the Supreme Court of New South Wales took the view that where a plaintiff suffered injuries in the course of committing a joint illegal activity with the defendant, the illegality could act to preclude the enforcement of an acknowledged right. Two cattle rustlers were in a truck transporting the stolen cattle to market when the driver fell asleep and the truck ran off the road, injuring the passenger. The plaintiff's claim for damages was defeated by a plea of illegality. Sugerman J said that the defence succeeded because the act complained of was "directly connected with the execution of the criminal purpose".[8] The court took a wide view of the scope of the joint illegal venture to include acts done in furtherance of the illegal purpose, here taking the cattle to market. Manning J said that it was important to distinguish between two separate problems: first, whether, regardless of the illegality, the facts gave rise to a duty of care on the part of the defendant towards the plaintiff; and secondly, if there was a duty which had been breached, whether the plaintiff's cause of action was so tainted by the illegality that public policy required the court not to lend its aid to enforce it.[9] Sugerman J was also of the view that the question was whether the plaintiff's illegality was such as to require a conclusion that it would be contrary to public policy to award damages for the injury.[10]

3.7 However, when the High Court of Australia first considered the issue of joint illegality in *Smith v Jenkins*[11] a different approach was adopted: the effect of illegality was not that the claim would be barred, as in *Godbolt v Fittock*, but rather that the illegality affected the relationship between the two parties and hence

---

[3] *Ibid*, at p 460.

[4] *Ibid*, at p 462.

[5] *Ibid*, at p 461.

[6] *Ibid*, at p 455.

[7] [1963] SR (NSW) 617.

[8] *Ibid*, at p 624.

[9] *Ibid*, at p 627.

[10] *Ibid*, at p 624.

[11] (1969) 119 CLR 397.

precluded any duty of care arising. The plaintiff and defendant assaulted a car owner and unlawfully took his vehicle. The plaintiff was the passenger and was injured in a subsequent car accident as a result of the defendant's negligence. The High Court unanimously held that the plaintiff was unable to recover damages. The exact ratio is unclear as the decision is supported by each judge in a different way, but the approach was in general one of denying the existence of any duty.

3.8 Barwick CJ decided first that the plaintiff should not succeed in his action and then went on to consider on what basis this could be placed.[12] As between persons jointly participating in a criminal act punishable by imprisonment, he concluded that the proper basis should be a refusal of the law to erect a duty of care as between such participants.[13] No duty of care arose between the plaintiff and the defendant as they did not stand in the relationship of passenger and driver but as joint participants in the very unlawful act out of which the injury arose.

3.9 Kitto J distinguished the instant case from that of *Henwood v The Municipal Tramways Trust (SA)*[14] on the basis that the latter was a case of unilateral illegality on the part of the injured person, and the question of whether the breach disentitled him to succeed depended on the true construction of the by-law. In contrast, the instant case involved a search not for statutory intention but rather the relevant general principle of common law. He held that in the present case the duty of care claimed was not one of a kind that flowed from a relationship created by lawful consensus. He considered that the governing principle was that persons committing an illegal act which they know - or must be presumed to know - to be unlawful have no legal rights *inter se* by reason of their respective participation in that act.[15]

3.10 Windeyer J considered that *ex turpi causa* was not a valid defence in tort and that it should be understood as being confined to contract.[16] He concluded that the question whether there was an action for negligence between criminals depended

---

[12] *Ibid*, at p 400.

[13] He rejected the option of deciding that the courts should refuse to lend their assistance to the recovery of damages for breach of a duty of care based on public policy, owing to the criminally illegal nature of the act out of which the harm arose.

[14] (1938) 60 CLR 438.

[15] (1969) 119 CLR 397, 403.

[16] See *per* Windeyer J *ibid*, at p 410:

> The intrusion of this Latin maxim into learned commentary, and also into judgments, has caused a confusion which would not have occurred if the writers had condescended to translation and had not taken the maxim into territory where it does not belong.

This dictum has been cited with approval in the combined judgement of Deane, Dawson, Toohey and Gaudron JJ in *Gollan v Nugent* (1988) 166 CLR 18, 46. Mason J also expressed the view that *ex turpi causa* has no place in the law of torts in *Jackson v Harrison* (1977-78) 138 CLR 438, 452.

on whether the negligence was so related to their unlawful conduct that the tort could be said to arise out of the crime - "but only in a general sense".[17]

3.11   Windeyer J thought that the terms, subject matter and purpose of the statute should be looked at, but considered that the question was whether the statute preserved a remedy which would otherwise be gone or recognised an exception to the rule that a criminal cannot have the aid of the law in his complaint against his fellow. He did not think the right approach was to ask whether the statute exhibits an intention to deprive one offender of a right of action against the other (the approach taken by Starke J as trial judge).[18]

3.12   Owen J concluded that no duty of care was owed on the basis that the law did not recognise those taking part in a joint criminal venture as "neighbours" in the sense in which Lord Atkin used the word in *Donoghue v Stevenson*.[19]

3.13   Walsh J thought that no right of action in negligence was given by the law in respect of the carrying out by one of the participants in a joint criminal enterprise of the particular criminal act in the commission of which they were engaged, the refusal to recognise that right being an application of the concept of public policy.

3.14   Later courts have grappled with the difficulties of the reasoning in *Smith v Jenkins* and have sought to explain the denial of duty as an inability or unwillingness on the part of the court to establish a standard of care,[20] or, more recently, on the basis that the illegality meant that the parties were not sufficiently proximate to establish a duty of care.[21]

3.15   In *Progress and Properties Ltd v Craft*[22] the plaintiff workman was injured when a hoist on which he was riding crashed to the ground, as a result of the operator's

---

[17]   (1969) 119 CLR 397, 421. Windeyer J continued:

> The question is whether the harm arose from the manner in which the criminal act was done. That question is not one of cause and consequence which can be answered in the old jargon of scholastic logic. Rather it is one of connexion [sic] and relationship and involvement. For that the modern jargon of remoteness and proximity is more useful.

He went on to state, *ibid*, at p 422:

> If two or more persons participate in the commission of a crime, each takes the risk of the negligence of the other or others in the actual performance of the criminal act. That formulation can be regarded as founded on the negation of duty, or on some extension of the rule *volenti non fit injuria*, or simply on the refusal of the courts to aid wrongdoers. How it be analysed and explained matters not.

[18]   *Ibid*, at p 424.

[19]   [1932] AC 562. Owen J considered it "odd" if a court could be called upon to consider and decide the standard of care to be expected of, eg, a prudent safebreaker and noted that a consistent approach was needed in contract and tort to prevent absurd results.

[20]   See *Progress and Properties Ltd v Craft* (1976) 135 CLR 651 and *Jackson v Harrison* (1977-78) 138 CLR 438.

[21]   See *Gala v Preston* (1991) 100 ALR 29.

[22]   (1976) 135 CLR 651.

negligence. The hoist was meant to carry goods not people, and a regulation made it an offence to ride on the hoist or permit someone else to do so. The High Court held[23] that there was a duty of care. Jacobs J gave the leading judgment. He considered that:

> A plea of illegality in answer to a claim in negligence is a denial that in the circumstances a duty of care was owed to the injured person. A duty of care arises out of the relationship of particular persons one to another. An illegal activity adds a factor to the relationship which may either extinguish or modify the duty of care otherwise owed. A joint illegal activity may absolve the one party from the duty towards the other to perform the activity with care for the safety of that other. That, it seems to me, is the effect of *Smith v Jenkins*.[24]

3.16 This meant that where the plaintiff had been involved in a joint illegal activity, the alleged negligent act may itself be a criminal act of a kind in respect of which a court would not be prepared to hear evidence for the purpose of establishing the standard of care which was reasonable in the circumstances.[25] However, such a principle would not apply as between two parties who contravened safety legislation. The relationship between the plaintiff's illegality and the operator's negligence did not require an examination of any special aspect of the relationship between the parties which could affect the standard of care, as, regardless of the illegality in operating the hoist, the same standard of care was expected of the operator.[26]

3.17 The 'no duty' analysis was further explained in *Jackson v Harrison*[27] by a similarly constituted High Court. The plaintiff was injured as a result of the defendant's negligent driving. Both parties' driving licences had been suspended in consequence of convictions for traffic offences and each was aware of the other's disqualification. Each of them had committed the offence of driving without a licence and aiding and abetting driving whilst disqualified. Despite the factual similarities to *Smith v Jenkins* it was considered by the majority[28] that these actions did not prevent the court assessing the standard of care.

3.18 Mason J said that if a plaintiff who was engaged in the performance of an illegal act could recover damages for the negligence of a defendant who was not involved in illegality, there was no evident reason why a plaintiff should be disentitled when

---

[23] Stephen, Mason, Jacobs and Murphy JJ; Barwick CJ dissenting. Jacobs J and Barwick CJ gave the only full judgments.

[24] (1976) 135 CLR 651, 668.

[25] The standard of care by a safebreaker was again given by way of example.

[26] In his dissenting judgment, Barwick CJ at (1976) 135 CLR 651, 655 argued that the relationship between the operator and the workman using the hoist was even closer than that of the two occupants of the car in *Smith v Jenkins*, and (*ibid*, at p 659) that the matter could not be resolved by looking for any indication in the regulation (agreeing with Windeyer J's approach in *Smith v Jenkins*).

[27] (1977-78) 138 CLR 438.

[28] Mason, Jacobs, Murphy and Aickin JJ.

he was injured in circumstances where both he and the defendant were together engaged in the commission of an illegal enterprise: that would place the 'innocent' party at a disadvantage.[29] He said it was incorrect to assert that *Smith v Jenkins* had decided that the participants in a joint illegal enterprise owe no duty of care to each other, and said that that case was limited to its particular facts, a variety of reasons being assigned to the decision.

3.19 In addition, Mason J was concerned that a broad reading of *Smith v Jenkins* would lead to foreseeability as the primary basis for determining a duty of care being discarded and thought that a more secure foundation for denying relief, though one more limited in application, was to say that the plaintiff must fail where the character of the enterprise was such that it was impossible for the court to determine the appropriate standard of care to be observed.[30]

3.20 Jacobs J (with whom Aickin J agreed) adhered to the views he had expressed in *Progress and Properties Ltd v Craft*[31] and based the defence upon a denial of a duty of care in the particular circumstances, rather than upon a denial of remedy for a breach of the duty of care.[32] To decline to permit the appropriate standard of care - and hence a duty - to be established, there had to be such a relationship between the negligent act and the nature of the illegal activity that a standard could only be determined by bringing into consideration the nature of the activities in which the parties were engaged.[33] He added that it was necessary in the case of a statutory offence to consider whether it was part of the purpose of the law offended against to disentitle the person from complaining of the other party's neglect: this purpose had to be clear.

3.21 Murphy J reached the same result but by a different route. He considered that the criticisms made by many commentators of the Australian approach to illegality in tort were valid and that there was a defect in the concept of the duty of care.[34] He thought that cases where joint participation in an illegal enterprise extinguishes the duty of care because the court cannot (as distinct from will not) determine an appropriate standard must be infrequent. He considered that *Smith v Jenkins* could not be properly understood as an instance where the court was unable to assess the standard of care owed. The standard of care owed to the plaintiff was the same as for every driver to drive carefully and not to injure their passengers. The denial of recovery there was simply an application of judicial policy. He concluded that in the instant case, although the illegality was serious, the legislation did not require that recovery be denied and that, apart from where there was a controlling statutory direction, recovery in negligence should not be

[29] (1977-78) 138 CLR 438.

[30] The detonation of an explosive device was an example of this, but the driving of a vehicle by an unlicensed and disqualified driver was not (so long as there was no agreement to drive recklessly).

[31] (1976) 135 CLR 651, 668.

[32] (1977-78) 138 CLR 438, 457.

[33] *Ibid.*

[34] *Ibid*, at p 462.

excluded because of illegality on the part of the plaintiff, either alone or jointly with the defendant.

3.22   Barwick CJ, dissenting, stated that when considering illegal joint ventures which were punishable by fine or imprisonment, a narrow view of the nature and scope of the activity should not be taken when applying the *Smith v Jenkins* principle. In his view, it should extend to cover all acts done to reap the benefits of the crime and perhaps acts indirectly connected with the accomplishment of the joint purpose.

3.23   More recently the High Court has recognised the deficiencies in adopting this 'standard of care' approach and has sought to distance itself from it, noting that:

> the legal principle which underlies the approach of the majority in *Progress & Properties v Craft* and *Jackson v Harrison* is not easy to discern.[35]

In *Gala v Preston*[36] the circumstances were similar to those in *Smith v Jenkins*[37] and *Jackson v Harrison*.[38] The plaintiff was injured in an accident involving a motor vehicle which he and the defendant had stolen whilst drunk. Although the High Court unanimously concluded that the plaintiff was owed no duty of care, as in *Smith v Jenkins*, they did not use the arguments advanced in *Smith v Jenkins* or in *Jackson v Harrison*.

3.24   Mason CJ, Deane, Gaudron and McHugh JJ gave the majority reasoning in a combined judgment and decided against the plaintiff on the basis that he was not in a relationship of "proximity" with the driver. The majority thought it necessary to take account of the developments in negligence and specifically, the development of the requirement of proximity in the duty of care. The requirement of proximity could take account of policy considerations and in cases of joint illegal enterprise it would be relevant to consider the appropriateness and feasibility of seeking to define the content of a relevant duty of care.[39] They concluded that in the "special and exceptional" circumstances of the case, the

---

[35] *Gala v Preston* (1991) 100 ALR 29, 47 *per* Brennan J. Mason CJ, Deane, Gaudron and McHugh JJ, who gave a combined judgment, also considered the ratio of *Smith v Jenkins* to be unclear.

[36] *Ibid.*

[37] (1969) 119 CLR 397.

[38] (1977-78) 138 CLR 438.

[39] (1991) 100 ALR 29, 36. They considered, eg, that it would border on the grotesque for the courts to seek to define the content of a duty of care owed by one bank robber to another in blowing up a safe which they were together seeking to rob; conversely, it would be unjust to deny the relationship of proximity between driver and passenger where the only passenger had encouraged the driver to drive momentarily in a lane reserved for vehicles with three or more occupants.

participants did not have a reasonable basis for expecting that the driver of the vehicle would drive it according to ordinary standards of competence and care.[40]

3.25 However, the members of the High Court were not unanimously persuaded of the merits of the "proximity" analysis. Brennan J strongly criticised the use of proximity in this extended sense and cited a passage from *Caparo v Dickman*,[41] in which Lord Bridge stated that proximity was not susceptible to precise definition and was merely a convenient label to attach to the features of different specific situations which the law recognised as pragmatically giving rise to the duty of care. He stated that there were few more familiar examples of a proximate relationship than that of driver and passenger, and thought that it was better to identify the consideration which negated the duty of care than simply to assert an absence of proximity. Brennan J considered that illegal acts could only prevent a duty of care arising on the basis that the policy of the statute precluded the existence of a duty of care in the circumstances, or that the courts would refuse to hear evidence from the plaintiff because of the illegality involved. Dawson and Toohey JJ dismissed the claim on other grounds.[42]

(3) The rationales for preventing recovery

3.26 It is difficult to discern the rationale or rationales behind the court refusing to erect a duty of care where the plaintiff is involved in illegality because in most cases no rationale is explicitly referred to. There are exceptions, however. First, in *Jackson v Harrison*,[43] Mason J sought to discredit a deterrence based rationale:

> The elimination of civil liability between the participants in a joint criminal enterprise cannot be sustained on the ground that it is a deterrent against criminal activity; it might with equal force be put forward as an inducement to such activity. Even if punishment of illegal conduct is not a matter for the exclusive attention of the criminal law, as I think it should be, a policy of deterrence directed against the participants in a joint criminal enterprise but not against the individual criminal makes very little sense.

3.27 Secondly, in *Gala v Preston*,[44] Dawson J undertook a review of the rationales. He considered that the rationale in illegality cases must be a refusal of the law to condone the commission of a criminal offence by granting a civil remedy. He did not think a rationale based on preserving the normative effect of the criminal law was persuasive because he did not think it possible to gauge the extent to which allowing a civil remedy might impair the normative and especially the deterrent

---

[40] The participants had been consuming massive amounts of alcohol - equivalent to forty scotches each - for some hours before the venture.

[41] [1990] 2 AC 605, 617-8.

[42] Dawson J thought that there was a "special element" in the relationship between the two people jointly engaged in the illegal use of the car, such that the law refused to set a standard - and hence a duty - of care. Toohey J thought the case indistinguishable from *Smith v Jenkins* (1969) 119 CLR 397.

[43] (1977-78) 138 CLR 438, 453

[44] (1991) 100 ALR 29, 53-54.

effect of the criminal law. He agreed with Mason J's judgment in *Jackson v Harrison*.[45] Dawson J thought that the rationale was that the court would refuse to impose a duty of care if it led to a "fundamental inconsistency" between the civil and the criminal law and also that it would be "wholly repugnant" to the accepted standards of the law if one participant in an illegal activity could ameliorate his position at the expense of the other in that situation.[46]

2. CANADA

(1) The Canadian approach

3.28 The Canadian system does recognise *ex turpi causa* as a defence in tort. However, the defence is rarely pleaded and even less often successfully invoked. It was not until the case of *Hall v Hebert*[47] that the Supreme Court of Canada made a definitive pronouncement on the validity and scope of the defence, the effect of which is that *ex turpi causa* "has been dealt an almost mortal blow."[48] We consider *Hall v Hebert* in detail, and our account of the law may start with this case, because, as McLachlin J (one of the judges[49]) explained, in Canada the defence has had a very chequered history:

> Appeal courts in Alberta and Manitoba have accepted that the doctrine can be applied in the tort context...[t]he Nova Scotia Court of Appeal has disagreed...[t]he British Columbia Court of Appeal has reached inconsistent decisions: *Mack v Enns* (1983) 44 BCLR 145, and *Betts v Sanderson Estate* (1988) 31 BCLR (2d) 1, deny the application of the doctrine in tort; the judgment of the Appeal Court in the case at bar says that doctrine applies, and that earlier judgments to the contrary are incorrect.[50]

It is little wonder then that Cory J noted that:

> [c]onsideration by the courts has been so inconsistent that it has given rise to a great deal of well merited criticism.[51]

3.29 In *Hall v Hebert*[52] the defendant car owner had allowed the plaintiff to roll-start his car down a hill when they were both intoxicated, which resulted in the plaintiff

---

[45] See above, para 3.26.

[46] (1991) 100 ALR 29, 54.

[47] [1993] 2 SCR 159.

[48] A Linden, *Canadian Tort Law* (6th ed 1997) p 494.

[49] The other members of the Supreme Court were La Forest, L'Heureux-Dubé, Iacobucci, Sopinka, Gonthier and Cory JJ.

[50] [1993] 2 SCR 159, 171. See also *Tallow v Tailfeathers* [1973] 6 WWR 732; *Teece v Teece v Honeybourn* [1974] 5 WWR 592; *Canada Cement LaFarge Ltd v British Columbia Lightweight Aggregate Ltd* [1983] 1 SCR 452; *Zickerfoose v Barotto Sports Ltd* 99 DLR (4th) 57; and *Norberg v Wynrib* [1992] 2 SCR 226.

[51] [1993] 2 SCR 159, 209.

[52] [1993] 2 SCR 159.

suffering serious head injuries. The Supreme Court[53] held, by a majority, that the defendant did owe the plaintiff a duty of care and the fact that the plaintiff was acting illegally did not act to negate that duty of care or bar the claim.[54]

3.30 The combined judgment of La Forest, L'Heureux-Dubé, McLachlin and Iacobucci JJ was delivered by McLachlin J. Her conclusions arose from a consideration of the historical uses of the power to deny recovery on the ground of illegal (or immoral) conduct and the doctrinal considerations underlying that power.[55]

3.31 She noted that the power expressed in the *ex turpi causa* maxim found its roots in the insistence of the courts that the judicial process should not be used for abusive, illegal purposes, and that the doctrine was well established in contract and insurance law. She also noted its chequered history in Canada in its application to tort, and referred to academic criticism, particularly where it was used to prevent recovery of compensatory damages for personal injury.[56] She then examined the cases with a view to determining whether a unifying theme or concern could be identified, sufficient to support the preservation of the maxim.

3.32 She thought that there was a clear need for the doctrine where to allow the tort claim would be to permit the plaintiff to profit from his or her wrong. She defined profit in a narrow sense, being a direct pecuniary reward for an act of wrongdoing.[57] Compensation for something other than wrongdoing, such as personal injury, would not amount to profit. However, she did not think that this concept explained fully why the courts had rejected claims in a number of cases she referred to.[58]

3.33 McLachlin J thought that a more satisfactory explanation was that allowing the claim would allow recovery for what is illegal:

> [Allowing recovery] would put the courts in the position of saying that the same conduct is both legal, in the sense of being capable of rectification by the court, and illegal. It would, in short, introduce an inconsistency in the law. It is particularly important in this context that we bear in mind that the law must aspire to be a unified

[53] On appeal from the Court of Appeal for British Columbia.

[54] Damages were reduced by 50% to account for the plaintiff's contributory negligence.

[55] [1993] 2 SCR 159, 170.

[56] McLachlin J cited B MacDougall, "*Ex turpi causa:* Should a Defence Arise from a Base Cause?" (1991) 55 Sask LR 1; G L Williams, *Joint Torts and Contributory Negligence* (1951); D Gibson, "Comment: Illegality of Plaintiff's Conduct as a Defence" (1969) 47 Can BR 89; E J Weinrib, "Illegality as a Tort Defence" (1976) 26 UTLJ 28; G H L Fridman, "The Wrongdoing Plaintiff" (1972) 18 McGill LJ 275.

[57] She referred to the situation in the Supreme Court case of *Canada Cement LaFarge Ltd v British Columbia Lightweight Aggregate Ltd* [1983] 1 SCR 452, where it was thought that it would be possible to use this principle to bar a claim based on the tort of conspiracy.

[58] McLachlin J referred to cases where claims by a burglar, a bookies' clerk, a vendor of illegal patent medicines, a fisherman using an illegal net, and an operator of an illegal gambling den had all been refused. See [1993] 2 SCR 159, 174-175.

institution, the parts of which - contract, tort, the criminal law - must be in essential harmony. For the courts to punish conduct with the one hand while rewarding it with the other, would be to 'create an intolerable fissure in the law's conceptually seamless web': Weinrib, *supra*, at p 42. We thus see that the concern, put at its most fundamental, is with the integrity of the legal system.[59]

3.34 McLachlin J went on to note that there may be cases where the principle of *ex turpi causa* should be invoked to prevent tort recovery where it did not involve profiting from wrongdoing. She referred to Professor Weinrib's article,[60] which suggested the defence should be available to prevent the "stultification of the criminal law" or "evasion of the consequences of the criminal law", and gave the example of a burglar suing his partner for damages for the cost of a fine which had been imposed when he had been caught and prosecuted owing to the partner's negligence. This would not be a claim for profit, but denying the claim would accord with the more fundamental rationale of the need to maintain internal consistency in the law, in the interest of promoting the integrity of the justice system.[61]

3.35 Summarising her views, McLachlin J said:

> [There] is a need in the law of tort for a principle which permits judges to deny recovery to a plaintiff on the ground that to do so would undermine the integrity of the justice system. The power is a limited one. Its use is justified where allowing the plaintiff's claim would introduce inconsistency into the fabric of the law, either by permitting the plaintiff to profit from an illegal or wrongful act, or to evade a penalty prescribed by criminal law. Its use is not justified where the plaintiff's claim is merely for compensation for personal injuries sustained as a consequence of the negligence of the defendant.[62]

3.36 Having explained the need for, and basis behind, the concept of *ex turpi causa* in tort, McLachlin J went on to counter the argument (advanced by Cory J[63]) that illegality should act to negate the existence of a duty of care:

> I am not sure that much is gained by replacing the defence of *ex turpi causa non oritur actio* with a judicial discretion to negate, or to refuse to consider, the duty of care. Shifting the analysis to the issue of duty provides no new insight into the fundamental question of when the courts should be entitled to deny recovery in tort to a plaintiff on the ground of the plaintiff's immoral or illegal conduct. Moreover, it introduces a series of new problems. In the end I fear it would prove

---

[59] *Ibid*, at p 176.

[60] E J Weinrib, "Illegality as a Tort Defence" (1976) 26 UTLJ 28.

[61] [1993] 2 SCR 159, 178.

[62] *Ibid*, at pp 179-180.

[63] See below, paras 3.43-3.46.

more problematic than has the defence of *ex turpi causa non oritur actio.*[64]

3.37 She thought that the 'duty' approach did not fully capture what was meant by the concept of *ex turpi causa.* Tort liability arose out of the relationship between the parties; the power of the court to deny recovery where it would undermine the coherence of the legal system, however, represented concerns independent of that relationship. She stated that policy concerns unrelated to the legal rules which governed the relationship between the parties have not generally been considered in determining whether a duty of care lies. As the legality or morality of the plaintiff's conduct was an extrinsic consideration to the relationship between the parties, for those rare cases where concerns for the administration of justice required the extrinsic characteristics of the plaintiff's conduct to be considered, it would be better to do it by way of defence, rather than distorting the notion of duty of care.[65]

3.38 There was no need to take the "rather novel step of positing judicial 'inability' to investigate the appropriate standard of care" instead of using the traditional concept of a defence to the action.[66] Tort law recognises many types of defence, some of which go to the relationship between the parties, as with the *volenti non fit injuria* defence, and others which are unrelated to that relationship, as with limitation periods. She saw no reason to treat *ex turpi causa* differently.

3.39 In addition, McLachlin J thought there were other problems with the 'duty' approach. First, if the question was one of duty, then the onus would be on the plaintiff to disprove the illegality in order to avoid a non-suit. Given the exceptional nature of the doctrine, it would be inappropriate to require the plaintiff to disprove illegality, rather than have the defendant prove it. Secondly, the 'duty' approach was an 'all-or-nothing' one that did not allow for selective application to a head of damage (for example, exemplary damages, or a claim for loss of future earnings based on an illegal occupation): this would not be a just approach. Thirdly, such an approach would raise procedural problems where there was a concurrent claim in contract and tort: the contract aspect would be dealt with by way of defence (and for the defendant to prove), but the tort aspect would be dealt with by way of duty (and for the plaintiff to disprove).

3.40 Applying the law to the facts, the four judges who gave the combined judgment held that the plaintiff's claim for damages for personal injury did not have to be prevented in order to maintain the internal consistency of the law (although the claim was reduced on the ground of contributory negligence).

3.41 Sopinka J, dissenting, thought that the plaintiff failed to establish that the defendant owed a duty to take care in the circumstances. He thought that whilst the lack of a reasonable expectation that the defendant would have an obligation to exercise care for the plaintiff's safety was not the proper basis for denying

---

[64] [1993] 2 SCR 159, 181.

[65] *Ibid*, at p 182.

[66] *Ibid*, at p 183.

recovery by reason of participation in criminal conduct, it was a material policy consideration relating to the existence of a duty of care. He thought that the *volenti non fit injuria* defence was an example of the application of such a policy to negate a duty of care. He thought that the concepts of *volenti non fit injuria* and *ex turpi causa* were examples of a definite policy not to recognise a duty of care in circumstances in which none could be expected.

3.42   Gonthier J, in a brief judgment, agreed with both McLachlin and Cory J that there was a duty of care, and that the defence of *ex turpi causa* did not apply on the facts, be it viewed as a defence or as a matter of public policy. He agreed that the defence of *ex turpi causa* was valid and had an important role to play in the limited circumstances to which it applied. He thought it reflected one facet of public policy which was best captured in the statement of its purpose made by Taylor J in *Mack v Enns*[67] and adopted by Sopinka J in *Norberg v Wynrib*:[68]

> The purpose of the rule today must be to defend the integrity of the legal system, and the repute in which the courts ought to be held by law-abiding members of the community.[69]

3.43   In contrast to the combined judgment of McLachlin, La Forest, L'Heureux-Dubé and Iacobucci JJ, Cory J took a different line of reasoning. He thought that there was much to be said for the view that apportionment legislation (on the grounds of contributory negligence) went far towards removing *ex turpi causa* as a defence, and thought that such a defence should be confined to the contractual sphere so far as possible.

3.44   Cory J thought that the proposition that a plaintiff should not profit from his wrong was more properly applicable to contract than to tort, given the prime purpose of tort law was compensation, although he thought that such a doctrine may be helpful in the sphere of "economic torts", where the plaintiff was essentially trying to recover the profit of its illegal bargain. However, he thought that this situation would properly be covered by the *volenti non fit injuria* defence, and did not need *ex turpi causa* to apply.[70]

3.45   He also rejected attempts to use *ex turpi causa* to reinforce the criminal law, as it would be unfair and unreasonable to impose a sanction beyond that which had been set out in the Criminal Code. On the concept of the integrity of the justice system, Cory J wondered whether the *ex turpi causa* defence was the best means of protecting the courts: he thought it would lead to arbitrary and personalised conclusions from the bench.[71] He also thought that:

---

[67]   (1981) 30 BCLR 337, 345.

[68]   [1992] 2 SCR 226, 316.

[69]   [1993] 2 SCR 159, 194.

[70]   The combined judgment of the majority suggested that it was not as clear as Cory J thought that a party entering into an illegal contract knowingly accepted the risks of the other party's breach. See *ibid*, at pp 173-174.

[71]   *Ibid*, at p 215.

compensation should not be looked upon as a judicial approbation of a plaintiff's illegal activities.[72]

3.46 Cory J thought that a better mechanism for assessing the actions of the plaintiff was either by means of contributory negligence, *volenti non fit injuria* or the consideration of a duty of care based on reasons of public policy. On the facts of the case he held that there was a clear duty owed by the defendant to the plaintiff, which had been breached. On the question of whether there was any reason of public policy to deny the plaintiff the right to recover all or part of his claim Cory J spoke in language reminiscent of the "public conscience" test used (and criticised) in English law:

> There is no reason why the [plaintiff] should be prevented from recovering compensation on the grounds of public policy. To permit him to recover would not offend or shock the conscience of reasonable right thinking members of the community fully apprised of the facts.[73]

(2) Summary

3.47 The combined judgment of McLachlin, La Forest, L'Heureux-Dubé and Iacobucci JJ in *Hall v Hebert* suggests that the *ex turpi causa* defence should be strictly confined and is generally inapplicable in cases of personal injuries. *Hall v Hebert* has been followed or referred to in a number of subsequent Canadian cases.[74] It additionally suggests a rationale for the defence which has not been discussed, so far as we are aware, in English cases. That rationale is the need for consistency within the law, and we think that it has considerable explanatory power not only for the Canadian cases, but also for many of the English cases. We return to this point in Part IV.

3. NEW ZEALAND

3.48 In New Zealand *ex turpi causa* is recognised as a general defence in tort. However, there is very little case law on this issue and it does not have a long history.[75] There are few cases on illegality in New Zealand and these take an essentially similar line to English law.[76] Given the existence of the Accident Compensation Scheme

---

[72] *Ibid*, at p 216.

[73] *Ibid*, at p 224. On the "public conscience" test, see above, paras 2.31-2.42.

[74] See *Ingles v Tutkaluk Construction Ltd* [2000] 1 SCR 298, where in an action for breach of contract and negligence relating to building renovation work, the Supreme Court held that it would be inconsistent with its jurisprudence to develop an area of negligence law where the conduct of the plaintiff was determinative of whether he or she was owed a duty of care, when that same court had specifically pronounced that a plaintiff's conduct may not be considered in determining whether a duty of care was owed in other areas of negligence law. In *Still v The Minister of National Revenue* [1998] 1 FC 549 the applicant was denied unemployment insurance benefits on the ground that her contract of service was illegal (she having no work permit). Referring to *Hall v Hebert*, the Federal Court held that it was not necessary to bar the claim in order to "preserve the integrity of the legal system". See also *Barr v Koldesk* (unreported) 17 October 1996 (SKQB).

[75] The earliest case found is from 1988.

[76] In *Tamworth Industries Ltd v Attorney-General* [1988] 1 NZLR 296 the Attorney-General argued that even a fortuitous finder of money, thought to be the proceeds of drug-dealing,

established in 1972, the dearth of personal injuries cases is perhaps unsurprising. The scheme provided benefits without requiring any proof of fault to persons suffering injury due to accident.[77] Its most significant feature is that it provided that where the scheme provided "cover" for a person suffering "injury by accident" the right to bring a civil action in tort for damages was abolished.[78]

3.49 The case of *Accident Compensation Corporation v Curtis*[79] is of interest because it examines the arguments for withholding compensation under the scheme from a wrongdoing accident victim. The two respondents were injured in unrelated car accidents, as a result of which each was convicted of dangerous driving causing death. They then applied to the Accident Compensation Corporation for compensation. The decision to deny lump sum compensation was overturned by the Accident Compensation Appeal Authority (ACAA). The High Court upheld the ACAA's decision. There was no question of whether a duty had arisen or had been negated but rather whether the injured claimants fell within or outside the statutory provision. The action in the Court of Appeal turned on the interpretation of section 26, concerning the scope and purpose of the Act, and section 92 of the Accident Compensation Act 1982,[80] which read:

> Where a person suffers personal injury by accident in the course of committing any criminal offence, and the injured person is convicted of the offence concerned, and sentenced to a term of imprisonment, cover shall exist but the Corporation may decline, in whole or in part, to give rehabilitation assistance and pay compensation if, in the opinion of the Corporation, it would be *repugnant to justice* for such

should be prevented from recovering it where it had been seized by the police in connection with a criminal charge. The Attorney-General argued that where the money could be connected with cannabis dealing by some unidentified person, the court ought not as a matter of public policy to lend its processes to enable a plaintiff to benefit from that unlawful activity. In a brief judgment, Cooke P reasoned that the possibility could not be ruled out that the majority shareholder of Tamworth, even if not himself guilty of drug-dealing, might have some knowledge of the drug-dealing. If so, it was possible that the money was tainted. However, there was no direct authority for or against the proposition that a windfall claim based on occupation should not prevail over the taint which should attach to the proceeds of serious criminal conduct. Cooke P was not prepared to say that the defence was not reasonably arguable and did not allow the defence of illegality to be struck out.

In the most recent case of *Brown v Dunsmuir* [1994] 3 NZLR 485, the public conscience test was used to reach a conclusion that the defence should be invoked to prevent the appellant's action in trespass against his neighbour when the neighbour placed soil on his property to prevent subsidence after the appellants had carried out an illegal excavation which had encroached onto the respondent's land. However, Penlington J received no argument on the basis of *Tinsley v Milligan* [1994] 1 AC 340.

[77] R S Miller, "An Analysis and Critique of the 1992 Changes to the New Zealand Accident Compensation Scheme" (1992) 5 Canterbury LR 1, 1.

[78] The scheme provided compensation for medical and rehabilitation expenses and for 80% of lost earnings so long as the disability continued. It also provided for a lump sum of up to $27,000 (NZ) for non-economic losses as well as other necessary expenses.

[79] [1994] 2 NZLR 519.

[80] Subsequently replaced by s 84 of the Accident Rehabilitation and Compensation Insurance Act 1992.

rehabilitation assistance to be given and such compensation to be paid.[81]

3.50   Fisher J, giving the judgment of the court, noted that the case concerned the principles upon which accident compensation should be refused where personal injury had been suffered in the course of criminal conduct. There was a presumption under section 92 that claimants would receive full rehabilitation assistance and compensation, but could lose those benefits if preconditions were satisfied[82] and a discretion was exercised adversely where cover would be "repugnant to justice". He noted that the Act was intended as a departure from the common law relating to *ex turpi causa*,[83] and that there would have to be an exceptional reason for departing from the dominant statutory objective of providing comprehensive no-fault cover.[84]

3.51   Fisher J concluded that given the purpose of the statute, it would not be repugnant to justice to award compensation. He considered that the principal considerations to be taken into account in exercising the discretion included: the gravity of the type of crime involved (including the maximum penalty for the offence); the personal culpability of the claimant; the impact of other burdens or penalties flowing from the criminal conduct, including the extent of the personal injury suffered in the course of committing the offence; the nature of the proposed statutory assistance and the plaintiff's needs and resources to meet them. In some situations, even where the plaintiff had suffered the penalty of imprisonment, the demands of retribution, denunciation, deterrence and reparation[85] could outweigh the general purpose of the statute but this threshold was a high one. In the instant case the court saw nothing objectionable in allowing rehabilitation assistance and lump sum compensation, and the appeal by the Corporation was dismissed.

3.52   The "repugnant to justice" test seems to direct the Corporation to take into account factors such as punishment[86] and deterrence but the New Zealand Court

---

[81]   Quoted at [1994] 2 NZLR 519, 520 (emphasis added).

[82]   The preconditions were that the claimant's personal injury must have been suffered in an accident which had occurred in the course of committing a criminal offence; that the claimant must have been convicted of the offence concerned; and that the claimant must have been sentenced to imprisonment.

[83]   [1994] 2 NZLR 519, 524.

[84]   Fisher J noted *ibid*, at p 525, that the Accident Compensation scheme was a form of self-funding social insurance to which all in the community contributed, and that the effect of invoking s 92 was to withhold from certain claimants the benefit of an insurance scheme to which they had already directly or indirectly contributed.

[85]   The latter four points being identified as underlying the sense of injustice contemplated by s 92. See *ibid*, at p 525.

[86]   Although note the comments of Fisher J *ibid*, at pp 526-527:

    In every case in which s 92 falls for consideration, the claimant will already have been fully punished by a conventional criminal Court. The offender has already paid his debt to society. Section 92 presupposes that in very limited circumstances, and in a very limited way, certain offenders can be penalised again but it is not a pretext for a second sentencing.

of Appeal has emphasised that it is not necessarily repugnant to justice to provide compensation to a person injured in the course of an illegal activity, and the threshold in the face of the initial statutory assumption that "cover shall exist" is a high one. To that extent at least it has something in common with the approach taken by the Canadian Supreme Court.

4. CIVIL LAW SYSTEMS

3.53   In *The Common European Law of Torts*, von Bar describes *ex turpi causa* as "[a] special case of voluntary assumption of risk".[87] Outside the context of English law, he gives few examples where *ex turpi causa* has been raised.[88] One, however, comes from Austria where the Austrian Supreme Court[89] concluded that where a person is "injured in a driving accident due to being the passenger despite knowing that the driver did not possess the necessary licence" the claimant has no claim to damages.[90] However, von Bar also comments that it would be wrong to assume that an offender loses all legal rights merely because of having committed a crime,[91] noting that in Spain the *Tribunal Supremo* has awarded full damages to the parents of a young offender who was killed by an overly eager guard, who was only supposed to call the police in the event of an alarm.

5. SCOTLAND

(1) The Scottish approach

3.54   Scots law recognises the defence of *ex turpi causa* in tort, although it is acknowledged as lying mainly in the area of contractual claims.[92] Several cases have used the maxim to conclude that no duty of care was owed between persons engaged in a "common criminal enterprise". Most of the cases involve passengers being injured in stolen or uninsured vehicles, and reference has been made to English and Australian decisions.

---

[87]   C von Bar, *The Common European Law of Torts: Volume Two* (2000) p 542, para 514.

[88]   See further van Gerven, *Cases, Material and Text on National, Supranational and International Tort Law* (2000) p 736, where it is stated that in general the defence of illegality will be raised only exceptionally - mainly when contributory negligence is, for one or another reason, not available. Van Gerven notes that in French law, the defence used to be raised against claims for "reflex damage" (*dommage par ricochet*) brought by concubines of the direct victim. The Cour de cassation changed this position in *Gaudras v Dangereux* (Cass Ch mixte, 27 February 1970) so that the defence is no longer admissible in this type of case. The defence is only available now in cases where to award compensation would lead in itself to an illicit or immoral result (see Cass civ 1re, 17 November 1983, *Groupe Drouot v Rumeau*). Similarly, in French law, where a plaintiff sues for loss of future earnings derived from an illegal or immoral activity, the defendant's illegality will only be exonerated if to award compensation would lead to an illicit or immoral act (see van Gerven, *Cases, Material and Text on National, Supranational and International Tort Law* (2000) p 737).

[89]   The Oberster Gerichtshof (OGH).

[90]   OGH 19 May 1994, ZVR 1995/41 (p 108), cited from C von Bar, *The Common European Law of Torts: Volume Two* (2000) p 542, para 514.

[91]   *Ibid*, at p 542, para 516.

[92]   *The Laws of Scotland, Stair Memorial Encyclopaedia* (1996) vol 15, para 411 at n 1.

3.55   In *Lindsay v Poole*[93] the pursuer was a passenger in a stolen car who was injured when the car crashed. He had been involved, with the defender, in the theft of the car. In the Outer House Lord Mayfield held that there was no duty of care owed by the driver to his passengers while all were participating in a joint and continuing illegal act. Reference was made to *Ashton v Turner*[94] and to *Smith v Jenkins*.[95] Lord Mayfield considered the circumstances of the latter to be essentially similar to the present case; there was a sufficient connection between the illegal act of taking the car away and the subsequent negligence of the defender as the accident occurred in the course of a continuing illegal act and close to the beginning of that act.

3.56   The sole instance in which the Inner House has considered *ex turpi causa* in tort is *Winnik v Dick*.[96] The pursuer had accepted a lift in the defender's car after a day's drinking and knew that the defender was drunk. There was a road accident and the pursuer was injured.[97] One of the defences raised was *ex turpi causa*.[98] The plea that the pursuer was a "joint participant in a criminal enterprise" with the drunken driver was dismissed, as that allegation was only raised at a late stage of an appeal and, in those circumstances, the Inner House declined to deal with it.[99] However, Lord Hunter stated that:

> It is clear, from the authorities cited to us, that the question whether two parties were participants in a joint criminal activity with the effect that one might in the circumstances be disabled from claiming reparation from the other is in a case like the present likely to be a question of fact and degree. Moreover, in such cases the matters of fact and degree may, as the authorities show, be relatively narrow.[100]

3.57   *Lindsay v Poole* has been followed in a number of cases. In *Sloan v Triplett*[101] a passenger injured in a road accident sought damages from the uninsured driver. It was held by Lord Allanbridge that the passenger had been involved in the theft of the car and the action was therefore unsuccessful. The same result was reached in *Wilson v Price*,[102] in which the pursuer merely knew that the driver was under age

---

[93]   1984 SLT 269.

[94]   [1981] 1 QB 137. See above, para 2.27.

[95]   (1969) 119 CLR 397. See above, paras 3.7-3.13.

[96]   1984 SLT 185.

[97]   The defender driver was convicted of an offence under the Road Traffic Act 1972.

[98]   A defence of *volenti non fit injuria* was held to be excluded by the wording of s 148(3) of the 1972 Act.

[99]   Damages had been reduced by 50% to take account of the pursuer's failure to use a seatbelt.

[100]   1984 SLT 185, 189.

[101]   1985 SLT 294.

[102]   1989 SLT 484.

and had taken the car without his father's permission. Lord Milligan held that this negated any duty of care.[103]

3.58 In contrast, in *Weir v Wyper*[104] the pursuer was a 16-year-old passenger who had been seriously injured through the defender's careless driving. The car driver argued that the passenger knew at the relevant time that he held only a provisional licence and was not being supervised and nonetheless asked him to drive her home, which he argued constituted a "common criminal activity". The passenger knew that the driver had only a provisional licence but stated that there had been a supervising driver present when she started the journey, but that he got out at a country lane and she was anxious to return home on that late night. The driver argued that *ex turpi causa* applied without the court having to consider the degree of criminality involved.

3.59 Lord Coulsfield held that Scots law did not have a firm rule that participation in any type of criminal conduct, however minor, barred a claimant from recovering damages: this depended on the particular facts and circumstances.[105] This was an approach which had been confirmed by the earlier decision of the Inner House in *Winnick v Dick*.[106] Lord Coulsfield considered that the reason it had been made a criminal offence for an unqualified driver to drive without supervision was to secure public safety and that the occurrence of an accident was precisely what the law requiring supervision was designed to prevent. He thought that it was not possible to take a blanket approach and say that every holder of a provisional licence must be taken to drive negligently or that all types of criminal activity should be viewed on the same footing. He concluded that the Scottish authorities, far from supporting the contention that Scots law had adopted a firm rule that participation in any type of criminal conduct, however minor, disabled an injured party from recovering damages, indicated that the matter is one of the particular facts.[107]

---

[103] A similar point was made in *Ashcroft's Curator Bonis v Stewart* 1998 SLT 163, where a passenger injured in a car accident sought damages from an uninsured driver. *Ex turpi causa* was raised on the basis that the passenger was involved with the driver in the joint criminal activity of taking and driving the motor vehicle without the owner's consent. The driver had been convicted of theft and the MIB maintained that they were not bound to satisfy any award of damages against the driver, alleging that the passenger knew or had reason to believe that the vehicle had been taken without the owner's consent. The defence did not succeed, as the evidence was insufficient to establish that the joint criminal activity had occurred or that the passenger had known that the vehicle had been unlawfully taken. However, Lord Cowie concluded that it was common ground between the parties that a person who suffers loss and injury through the negligence of another cannot recover damages from that other if, at the time of the negligent act, the injured party was participating with the other person in a joint criminal activity. Reference was made to *Lindsay v Poole* 1984 SLT 269.

[104] 1992 SLT 579.

[105] *Ibid*, at pp 581-2.

[106] 1984 SLT 185, 189.

[107] 1992 SLT 579, 581.

3.60 In his judgment Lord Coulsfield referred to both *Smith v Jenkins*[108] and *Jackson v Harrison*,[109] citing the judgment of Mason J in the latter case to show that a rule of absolute application would be too draconian to be acceptable. He concluded that in the instant case the pursuer was neither participating in any significant criminal activity nor that any reasonable application of public policy would deny her a right to recover damages for injuries caused by the defender's negligent driving.[110]

3.61 This case was followed in *Taylor v Leslie*.[111] A car passenger was killed in a road accident on a remote island as a result of the defender's negligent driving. The deceased, having borrowed a friend's car,[112] allowed his 16-year-old friend, who was unlicensed and uninsured, to drive the car without the owner's knowledge and consent. The deceased's parents brought an action against the driver who raised the *ex turpi causa* defence on the basis that they were both participating in a common criminal activity. Judge Wheatley QC rejected the defence. He relied on the previous authority that whether *ex turpi causa* applied was dependent on the facts and circumstances of the case and stated that in that remote community the negligent driver's illegal conduct would not have been considered particularly reprehensible. This reasoning has led one commentator to note how vague the criteria can be and that this may lead to questionable factors being taken into account.[113]

(2) Summary

3.62 Scots law has drawn on the position in English and Australian law. The Scots law position seems to be essentially similar to English law in that claims have been denied when the joint criminal activity has appeared to be serious[114] and have been allowed when it was not, although the pursuer's award may be reduced on account of his or her contributory negligence.[115] The Inner House has only considered the defence on one occasion and clearly stated in that case that it was not prepared to lay down a blanket rule preventing injured wrongdoers from suing their fellow participants in a common criminal enterprise. Rather it considered that the

---

[108] (1969) 119 CLR 397.

[109] (1977-78) 138 CLR 438.

[110] 1992 SLT 579, 583.

[111] 1998 SLT 1248.

[112] With the owner's consent.

[113] It has been argued that adopting the approach of *Taylor v Leslie* literally would require one to ascertain the degree to which the particular community in which the conduct took place considered it to be reprehensible so the defence would be "location-driven" and inappropriate. Here it was considered that the appropriate outcome was achieved but the reasoning was open to question. See B J Rodger, "*Ex turpi*: A Location-driven Defence?" [1998] Jur Rev 201.

[114] Though it may be questioned whether the conduct in *Wilson v Price* 1989 SLT 484 (see above, para 3.57) would be viewed by all courts as sufficiently serious for the defence to apply.

[115] See *Winnik v Dick* 1984 SLT 185, *Ashcroft's Curator Bonis v Stewart* 1998 SLT 163, *Weir v Wyper* 1992 SLT 579 and *Taylor v Leslie* 1998 SLT 1248.

decision to allow recovery to be one of fact and degree.[116] The rationale underlying the *ex turpi causa* defence has not been discussed fully in a Scots case, though it was given some examination in *Weir v Wyper*.

6. CONCLUSION

3.63   The Australian cases have highlighted the difficulties involved in using the duty of care mechanism in all cases to consider issues of illegality in tort actions and the need to consider *ex turpi causa* as a relevant defence in tort. This approach is one we would not recommend.[117]

3.64   The Canadian decision in *Hall v Hebert*[118] may be of assistance to the English courts, given its close examination of the possible justifications for the defence. In Part IV of this paper we discuss what we consider to be the explanatory power of "consistency" as a rationale.

3.65   The Supreme Court of Canada's approach does appear more generous to the person who has suffered personal injuries through the defendant's negligence when the plaintiff was involved in some illegal activity. Kostal argues[119] that by comparing recent case law on illegality in tort in the two jurisdictions a significant divergence of judicial opinion on the proper ambit of the duty of care can be seen. He considers that the Australian cases reflect the more general aim shown in Australian law of narrowing the scope of liability in negligence which he describes as "openly hostile to an expansive liability in negligence." He contrasts this with the Canadian position, which he calls "overwhelmingly favourable to expansive liability". We will return to the question of this type of case when we have considered the policy rationales underlying the illegality defence.[120]

---

[116] *Winnik v Dick, ibid*, at p 189. See above, para 3.56.

[117] See below, paras 5.16-5.18.

[118] [1993] 2 SCR 159.

[119] R Kostal, "Currents in the Counter-Reformation: Illegality and duty of care in Canada and Australia" [1995] Tort LR 100.

[120] See below, paras 4.82-4.98.

PART IV
POLICY RATIONALES UNDERLYING THE DOCTRINE OF ILLEGALITY

1. INTRODUCTION

4.1 In Part I of this paper we said that we believe it to be important that the application of the illegality defence in tort cases be linked clearly to the policy rationales underlying the doctrine.[1] If this is not done there is a danger that the application will be, or will appear to be, arbitrary and unpredictable. A defence which operates arbitrarily to deprive claimants of what otherwise would be their remedies may infringe their Convention Rights under the Human Rights Act 1998.[2] It is therefore important to identify the policy rationales underlying the defence.

4.2 One of the difficulties involved in identifying the policies that underlie the doctrine of illegality, particularly as it operates in tort, is that many cases are silent on the point. Some merely state the rules of the doctrine, or their effect, without considering *why* those rules exist, or at least leaving that point to be dealt with by implication; others explain the rules as if they provide the justification.[3]

4.3 In Consultation Paper No 154 we referred[4] to Lord Mansfield's comments in *Holman v Johnson*[5] and examined why it is that, in cases of contracts and trusts that are tainted by illegality, the court will not "lend its aid to a man who founds his cause of action upon an immoral or an illegal act".[6] Lord Mansfield's statement is not, of course, the rationale in itself. First, it will not explain all the cases: a claimant whose claim is closely connected to his or her illegal act may be defeated by the illegality doctrine even though he or she does not have, in a technical sense, to found the claim upon it.[7] Secondly, it is not self-explanatory in the sense that it does not tell us *why* the court will not lend its aid to a claim founded on an immoral or an illegal act.

4.4 In this part we endeavour to establish what have been suggested as rationales for the defence in tort cases, and examine whether these rationales are supportable. We conclude provisionally, first, that the rationales which we put forward in Consultation Paper No 154 as supporting the doctrine in contract and trusts cases are not sufficient to explain all the tort cases; secondly, that most cases can be

---

[1] See above, paras 1.8-1.9.

[2] See above, paras 1.5-1.8.

[3] Eg, to show that there is a close causal link between the illegal act and the claim does not explain *why* the claim should be barred.

[4] At para 6.2.

[5] (1775) 1 Cowp 341; 98 ER 1120.

[6] (1775) 1 Cowp 341, 343; 98 ER 1120, 1121.

[7] See, eg, *Cross v Kirkby, The Times* 5 April 2000.

explained by a further rationale which we term "consistency"; but, thirdly, that it is hard to see the rationale for some statements of the defence. With one exception, we think that the actual outcomes of all the English cases to date can be defended, but not necessarily on the grounds of illegality.[8]

4.5 The rationales which we considered in Part VI of Consultation Paper No 154 were: (1) upholding the dignity of the courts; (2) the plaintiff should not profit from his or her own wrongdoing; (3) deterrence, and (4) punishment. We stated in the consultation paper that all four policies had merit, and concluded that together they showed the need to retain an illegality doctrine of some kind.[9]

4.6 In Consultation Paper No 154 we did not ask consultees to comment directly on whether or not they agreed with the main policy rationales as we had explained them. However, several of those who responded to that consultation paper did question the appropriateness or effectiveness of one or more of those policy rationales, although a majority accepted our analysis without comment.

4.7 We noted in Part II of this paper that the use of the illegality doctrine in tort is a recent practice compared to its use in contract.[10] It is partly because of this, and partly because its provenance has been questioned by several commentators, that our examination of the law in this area resulted in more focused and detailed attention being given to the reasons behind the existence of the doctrine in tort than we gave to contract and trusts law in Consultation Paper No 154. As part of this reappraisal of the rationales for the existence of the doctrine we have come to revise our position with respect to some of the rationales that we advanced in that consultation paper. We have come to the provisional conclusion that one of the arguments advanced in the consultation paper in support of the operation of the doctrine, that of punishment, should no longer be regarded as a valid argument to inform our general reform strategy, whether it be for contract, trusts or tort. We also asked ourselves whether it is possible to combine these areas into one set of policies. We think it would be useful if this could be achieved, and will return to this point later in the paper.[11]

2. THE POLICY RATIONALES

4.8 The illegality doctrine in tort has been justified in the reported cases - either explicitly or implicitly - on several policy bases. These include some of the rationales discussed in Consultation Paper No 154 in relation to contract and trusts: (1) the need to preserve the dignity and reputation of the courts and legal system; (2) the need to deter unlawful or immoral conduct, and (3) the need to prevent a claimant profiting or benefiting from his or her own wrongdoing. The fourth policy discussed in that paper, punishment, has been raised in relation to

---

[8] The exception being *Meah v McCreamer* [1985] 1 All ER 367. See above, para 2.6.

[9] Consultation Paper No 154, para 6.12. We rejected the simple option of dispensing with any special rules for illegal transactions, a view which met with virtually unanimous support from consultees.

[10] See above, para 2.1.

[11] See below, paras 6.52-6.54.

tort by some academic commentators.[12] We think that these rationales are not all of equal strength, and some are of very limited application. In the sections that follow we examine each of these rationales.

4.9   We then consider three further possible rationales, namely that the court should not appear to condone or encourage the claimant's criminal or illegal conduct, "consistency", and "responsibility". We end by discussing two particular classes of case, that of claimants injured during the course of some illegal activity, and that where the claimant does not have to rely on his or her illegality, in the light of the various rationales.

(1) Rejection of punishment

(i) Report No 247, Aggravated, Exemplary and Restitutionary Damages

4.10   In our Report on Aggravated, Exemplary and Restitutionary Damages[13] we considered punishment from the point of view of justifying an increased award of damages against a defendant. One of the criticisms of "punishment" in a civil context considered in that Report was that it confused the civil and criminal functions of the law.[14] We there answered that criticism[15] on the basis that the principled case for retaining exemplary damages began with the proposition that civil punishment was a different type of punishment to that of criminal punishment, and we thought that the civil form of punishment did not necessarily have to mimic the criminal form.[16]

4.11   In distinguishing civil punishment from criminal punishment we said:

> Two distinctive features of civil punishment are relied on. The first concerns the *locus standi* or entitlement to sue of complainants. Civil punishment is sought and enforced by individual victims of wrongdoing. In contrast, criminal punishment is sought by or on behalf of the state: even though an individual can bring a private prosecution, he or she will be regarded as acting on behalf of the state. The second concerns the stigma associated with criminal punishment...£10,000 exemplary damages for assault would be less drastic than a £10,000 fine and criminal record for the same assault.[17]

---

[12]   See, eg, R A Buckley, "Law's Boundaries and the Challenge of Illegality" in R A Buckley (ed), *Legal Structures* (1996) ch 9, pp 234-235. It has been suggested that preventing a wrongdoer benefiting from his wrong (see below, paras 4.36-4.47) is part of the rationale of punishment (see eg, P Jaffey, *The Nature and Scope of Restitution*, 2000 p 222). However, we see denial of benefit as a policy argument separate from that of punishment. Cf the position in New Zealand, where a punitive rationale appears to be part of the statutory intention behind the power to withhold compensation under what used to be s 92 of the Accident Compensation Act 1982. See above, para 3.51.

[13]   Law Com No 247.

[14]   *Ibid*, at paras 5.16-5.19.

[15]   For detailed consideration of the arguments, see *ibid*, at paras 5.20-5.25.

[16]   *Ibid*, at paras 5.20-5.25.

[17]   *Ibid*, at para 5.23.

We took the view in that Report that in the face of the above arguments, the objections[18] to exemplary damages fell away.

4.12 We concluded in our Report that the case for retaining exemplary damages was to be preferred to the case for abolition, and that civil punishment had an important and distinctive role to play.[19] The argument was regarded as finely balanced, and other arguments of general policy were detailed to support that view.[20]

(ii) Consultation Paper No 154

4.13 In the consultation paper we considered whether punishment was a valid argument supporting the doctrine of illegality. After noting that it was not frequently referred to in the case law, and noting that in our Report on Aggravated, Exemplary and Restitutionary Damages[21] we saw no reason in principle why punishment should not also be regarded as an aim of the civil law, we stated that we accepted that a legitimate aim of the illegality rules may be to punish the plaintiff for his or her obnoxious behaviour.[22]

4.14 Few consultees made specific comments on our analysis of these policies, although some expressed general support, and one made specific comments against punishment being used in the civil law.[23]

(iii) Our current view

4.15 The argument that it is justifiable to deny a civil claim as a punishment for illegal behaviour has been the subject of criticism, particularly given its arbitrary and potentially disproportionate nature.[24] In the context of illegality, we accept the force of these criticisms.

---

[18] Outlined in Law Com No 247, para 5.21.

[19] *Ibid*, at para 5.25.

[20] *Ibid*, at para 5.27. However, none of these arguments we consider to have significant application to the law of illegality. The Government accepted the recommendations on aggravated and restitutionary damages that we made in the Report. In the absence of a clear consensus on the contending arguments for a complete legislative overhaul of exemplary damages or abolition, the Government decided not to take forward our proposals for legislation on exemplary damages. See Written Answer, *Hansard* (HC) 9 November 1999, vol 337, col 502.

[21] Law Com No 247.

[22] Consultation Paper No 154, para 6.11.

[23] This consultee made reference to the European Continental principle of *nulla poene, sine lege*. He also referred, in the context of restitution, to the German courts having displaced the punishment doctrine with the "so-called *Rechtsschutzversagung* theory", whereby denial of a restitutionary remedy is justified by the plaintiff having placed himself outside the legal order. This, of course, has been rejected in English law: see above, para 1.25.

[24] See, eg, J Shand, "Unblinkering the Unruly Horse: Public Policy in the Law of Contract" [1972A] CLJ 144, 148-150; J Wade, "Benefits Obtained Under Illegal Transactions - Reasons For and Against Allowing Restitution" (1946) 25 Texas LR 31, 35-36.

4.16 Our Report on Aggravated, Exemplary and Restitutionary Damages[25] was dealing with the case for retaining the court's power to award exemplary damages against a defendant, and we think that such a justification is appropriate in that context. We explained that "[c]ivil punishment is sought and enforced by individual victims of wrongdoing."[26] However, this situation in respect of exemplary damages is different from that where punishment is sought to be used to support the existence of the illegality doctrine.

4.17 First, invoking the defence of illegality would not involve civil punishment being sought and enforced by an "individual victim of wrongdoing". It is generally invoked by the *defendant*,[27] who cannot always be seen as the victim of wrongdoing,[28] and who, as a tortfeasor, contract breaker or betrayer of trust, is not "innocent" in the way that a claimant seeking exemplary damages is. Any "windfall" involved in barring the claim on a punitive basis may go to a defendant who is not innocent in civil law terms, and who does not have to pay out in damages for his or her wrongdoing. Moreover, quite apart from having committed the alleged tort, the defendant may also be a participant in the claimant's crime.

4.18 Secondly, whilst the stigma of punishment is less in a civil context, the disproportionate effect of that punishment in the context of illegality does concern us: exemplary damages operate so as to vary the amount of the damages the defendant would have to pay in any event as a consequence of his or her tort, and can be set at a level proportionate to the wrong; illegality normally deprives the claimant of a whole cause of action. We noted in the consultation paper:

> [Punishment] is not a policy that can be easily pursued by the present strict illegality rules. The simple refusal of civil relief is generally a very arbitrary and blunt method of meting out punishment, since the penalty is not in any way tailored to fit the illegality involved.[29]

4.19 In light of the above considerations, we now think that it is inappropriate to use the arguments advanced in the Report to justify punishment as a rationale for denying a cause of action in the way that we originally sought to do in Consultation Paper No 154.[30]

4.20 In addition to these considerations, we also question the need for a rationale of punishment in the context of illegality. We consider that many situations which at

---

[25] Law Com No 247.

[26] *Ibid*, at para 5.23. See above, para 4.11.

[27] Although the court is probably able to raise the matter of its own motion. See above, para 2.2 n 8.

[28] Particularly where the victim of the claimant's crime and the defendant are two different entities, such as in those cases where the claimant is seeking an indemnity for the consequences of his or her criminal action.

[29] Consultation Paper No 154, para 7.41.

[30] We also note that our proposals in the Report expressly excluded the availability of punitive damages in the context of breach of contract, or for negligence other than exceptional cases. See Law Com No 247, paras 5.49-5.52.

first glance might appear to support the assertion that punishment should be a rationale in support of illegality can be satisfactorily covered by other policy rationales, without the need to invoke a punitive basis. Not allowing a claimant to benefit from his or her crime would be sufficient justification to prevent a hired assassin suing for unpaid fees,[31] as it would be for depriving highwaymen of their right to sue one another for a share in their ill-gotten gains.[32] Neither of these cases requires a rationale of civil "punishment" to explain what may be seen as a "just" result, nor do we think it is required by any other situation that arises in the case law.

(iv) The need to avoid "double punishment"

4.21 Rather, we think that the court should consider whether a denial of the claim may have an unduly punitive effect. In the consultation paper we noted that:

> clearly there will be a risk of "double punishment" where the plaintiff
> has already been convicted of a criminal offence or made to pay
> damages for a legal wrong in respect of the same conduct.[33]

4.22 As a result, we went on to consider provisionally that the court should take into account whether the penal effect of denying the plaintiff relief was proportionate to the illegality involved. We thought that where the illegality was trivial but the value of the benefits conferred by the plaintiff on the defendant was vast, denying a restitutionary claim might be an excessive penalty. "Double punishment" might also be regarded as disproportionate. In the light of this, it is necessary to ensure that, even if there is no distinct policy of punishment, the impact of the other policies does not have a punitive effect.

4.23 Whilst we provisionally propose later in this paper to create a structured discretion that requires proportionality between the illegality involved and the effect of denying relief,[34] and to that extent the risk of disproportionate punishment is reduced, we do not consider that this step in itself justifies a rationale of punishment supporting the doctrine of illegality.

4.24 **Our provisional view is that punishment does not provide a sufficient rationale for the existence of the doctrine of illegality, and that therefore the court should only allow the illegality defence where it can be justified on policy rationales other than punishment. We ask consultees whether they agree with our rejection of punishment as a rationale for the doctrine of illegality.**

[31] See R A Buckley, "Law's Boundaries and the Challenge of Illegality" in R A Buckley (ed), *Legal Structures* (1996) ch 9, p 230.

[32] See *Everet v Williams* (1725) reported at (1893) 9 LQR 197.

[33] Consultation Paper No 154, para 7.41.

[34] See below, para 6.29.

(2) The need to preserve the dignity and reputation of the courts and legal system

4.25 In Consultation Paper No 154 we examined the argument that the court should be able in some cases to be free from stooping to the indignity of inquiring into the relative merits and demerits of the parties and leave matters as they are. We considered that the "dignity of the courts" policy rationale had merit, but we noted that the confines of that rationale should also be recognised.[35] We thought that the dignity of the court could only be at risk where the transaction involved particularly serious illegality. One consultee expressly agreed with us on this point, but there were few other comments on this policy from consultees.

4.26 We think that, in practice, successful recourse to this rationale in tort actions will be very rare. The few reported cases where the defence of illegality has succeeded on this basis arise mainly out of contractual actions (and these are of some age[36]). The tort cases often involve claims being brought by claimants who have committed serious offences,[37] yet the courts have not felt their dignity in need of protection when hearing these claims and in some cases the claims have been allowed[38] or other reasons have been used to bar the claim instead.[39] The circumstances of a tort case in which the court would feel compelled to protect its dignity are likely to be very extreme, and therefore rare.[40] However, we accept that there may be *exceptional* circumstances where this is the case, and to this extent we do not seek to deny the validity of this rationale entirely (as we have sought to do with punishment earlier in this section).

---

[35] Consultation Paper No 154, para 6.6.

[36] See, eg, *Everet v Williams* (1725) reported at (1893) 9 LQR 197 (the "Highwayman's case"); *Tappenden v Randall* (1801) 2 Bos & Pul 467, 471; 126 ER 1388, 1390; and the judgment of Lush J in *Parkinson v College of Ambulance Ltd and Harrison* [1925] 2 KB 1, 13.

[37] See, eg, *Meah v McCreamer* [1985] 1 All ER 367; *Meah v McCreamer and others (No 2)* [1986] 1 All ER 943; and *Webb v Chief Constable of Merseyside Police* [2000] QB 427 (in which the claimant had not been convicted of an offence but the Recorder had held that, on the balance of probability, the money was the proceeds of drug dealing). The House of Lords was willing to hear the claim in *Tinsley v Milligan* [1994] 1 AC 340 (a trusts case), despite both parties having been involved in a fraud on the Revenue, but that fraud was not treated as serious.

[38] See, eg, *Webb v Chief Constable of Merseyside Police, ibid.*

[39] See, eg, *Clunis v Camden and Islington Health Authority* [1998] QB 978, where, despite the serious offence of manslaughter having been committed, no mention was made of outraged dignity by the Court of Appeal in its decision to bar the claim.

[40] It may be possible to argue that the court in *Hegarty v Shine* (1877-82) 14 Cox CC 145 felt that it was beneath its dignity to consider the cause of action, see the comments of Deasy LJA *ibid*, at p 152:

> For two days a most able judge and a jury have been engaged in investigating the details and occasions of this course of immorality, in order to discover whether the probable consequence of that course of immorality [venereal disease] did actually originate from it. I am of the opinion that such an investigation is no fit subject for the attention of a Court of Justice, and that no such investigation ought to receive judicial sanction.

No doubt the outrage of the court merely reflects a different set of social values then operating. We doubt whether the result would be the same today.

4.27   It is our provisional view, therefore, that preserving the dignity of the courts may provide a justification for applying the doctrine of illegality in tort cases but only in unusual or extreme circumstances. We ask whether consultees agree with us.

(3) The need to deter unlawful or immoral conduct

4.28   In the consultation paper we referred to the frequently mentioned policy rationale of deterring unlawful or immoral conduct,[41] and thought that it should be an important one underlying the illegality doctrine. However, following the publication of that paper, several consultees questioned the value of this policy rationale, and whether there was real deterrent effect. Does this policy rationale remain a valid one, and does it have any application to the law of tort?

4.29   Deterrence has certainly been given as a rationale for the doctrine in the contract and trusts cases - see the reference by Lord Goff in his speech in *Tinsley v Milligan*[42] to the words of Ralph Gibson LJ in the Court of Appeal:

> In so far as the basis of the *ex turpi causa* defence, as founded on public policy, is directed at deterrence it seems to me that the force of the deterrent effect is in the existence of the known rule and in its stern application. Lawyers have long known of the rule and must have advised many people of its existence. It does not stop people making arrangements to defraud creditors, or the revenue, or the DSS.[43]

However, the deterrence argument was also criticised in that same case.[44] We also note the criticism of the deterrence argument made by Mason J in the Australian (tort) case of *Jackson v Harrison*,[45] that as between participants in joint illegality, knowledge that the other could not make a claim could equally be an inducement to crime.

4.30   In tort cases what may be a deterrence argument is sometimes expressed as not encouraging the claimant or others. For example, in *Thackwell v Barclays Bank Ltd*[46] Hutchison J accepted submissions that the defence was available:

---

[41]   Consultation Paper No 154, paras 6.9-6.10.

[42]   [1994] 1 AC 340, 363.

[43]   [1992] Ch 310, 334.

[44]   See the comments of Lord Lowry in the House of Lords at [1994] 1 AC 340, 368:

> I am not impressed by the argument that the wide principle acts as a deterrent to persons in A's position. In the first place, they may not be aware of the principle and are unlikely to consult a reputable solicitor. Secondly, if they commit a fraud, they will not have been deterred by the possibility of being found out and prosecuted. Furthermore, the wide principle could be a positive encouragement to B, if he is aware of the principle, because by means of his complicity, he may become not only the legal owner but the beneficial owner.

[45]   (1977-78) 138 CLR 438, 453. See above, para 3.26.

[46]   [1986] 1 All ER 676. See above, para 2.10.

where the court, in finding for the plaintiff, would be indirectly assisting or encouraging the plaintiff in his criminal, fraudulent or illegal activity.[47]

4.31 We think deterrence does remain a rationale for illegality both generally and in tort, but we are less convinced of its importance in this latter area. The force of deterrence would seem to us greater where, for example, two parties knowingly enter into an agreement to perform an illegal act, than when someone is contemplating an illegal act in the course of which he or she might be injured by another's fault, or might suffer some loss.

4.32 In some of the reported tort cases, the illegality which is in issue for the civil claim stems from the commission of a serious criminal offence against life[48] or road safety.[49] If the deterrent effect of the criminal sanctions that go along with those offences is not sufficient to prevent the commission of similar offences by others, then we find it difficult to say that preventing any civil claim that subsequently arises will add to that deterrent effect or be a more effective one.[50]

4.33 However, we accept that there may be some circumstances in tort where it would be proper for the court to rely on deterrence as a reason for barring the claim, particularly in those situations where the results of illegal behaviour on such a claim would be more likely to be known to those who might be likely to break the law, or where there is perhaps an overlap between the tortious claim and a contractual one.

4.34 Several cases suggest that it is important that the court is not seen to condone serious illegality.[51] We are uncertain when judges talk of "not condoning" the activity or "not encouraging" others whether they mean this as part of the need to deter such conduct, or whether this is seen as a separate rationale. We return to this point shortly.

4.35 **It is our provisional view that deterrence will sometimes, but only rarely, provide a justification for applying the doctrine of illegality in tort cases. We ask whether consultees agree with us.**

---

[47] *Ibid*, at p 689. Nicholls LJ said that he would add the words "or encouraging others in similar criminal acts" to this sentence, when discussing this case in *Saunders v Edwards* [1987] 1 WLR 1116, 1132.

[48] See, eg, *Clunis v Camden and Islington Health Authority* [1998] QB 978 (manslaughter). See above, para 2.7.

[49] See, eg, *Pitts v Hunt* [1991] 1 QB 24 (reckless/drunken driving). See above, para 2.4.

[50] See the comments of Diplock LJ in *Hardy v Motor Insurers' Bureau* [1964] 2 QB 745, 770:

> It seems to me to be slightly unrealistic to suggest that a person who is not deterred by the risk of a possible sentence of life imprisonment from using a vehicle with intent to commit grievous bodily harm would be deterred by the fear that his civil liability to his victim would not be discharged by his insurers.

[51] See above, paras 2.63-2.67.

(4) The need to prevent a claimant profiting from his or her own wrongdoing

4.36 In Consultation Paper No 154 we accepted the value of this rationale, and believed that the illegality rules in relation to contract and trusts had an important role to play in enforcing it. We noted that this policy rationale has wider application than just that of supporting the illegality doctrine.[52] However, we also recognised that the rule should not apply to wholly innocent parties.[53] We maintain these views, and consider that to argue that this rationale should not exist would be inconsistent with those (mainly criminal) provisions of the law that seek to prevent, deter or punish the behaviour from which the claimant is seeking to profit. For the law to proscribe particular conduct and yet allow the offender successfully to sue to ensure that he or she profits from that conduct is, we believe, an unacceptable situation, and one that would, in effect, undermine the law.[54] It would have the result that to allow someone to benefit from his or her wrongdoing would mean that "crime would pay".

4.37 In contract law it is relatively easy to see instances of this principle in operation within the case law.[55] We have no doubt that the policy of preventing the claimant profiting from his or her wrongdoing may also underlie some of the reported tort cases: in *Thackwell v Barclays Bank Ltd*,[56] for example, the plaintiff claimed damages in negligence and conversion in respect of a cheque which represented the proceeds of a fraud in which the plaintiff had knowingly participated. The claim failed for reasons of illegality, Hutchison J holding that permitting the plaintiff to recover the proceeds of the cheque would have the effect of indirectly assisting in the commission of a crime.[57]

4.38 We noted in Part II of this paper that a number of cases that involved illegality were not claims for "profit" as such, but rather were seeking damages relating to compensation for the time the claimant had spent in prison or a secure hospital, or a form of indemnity to pay for the damages awarded to the victims of the claimant's crimes. Moreover, several cases were barred on the grounds of illegality where the claim was for personal injuries, but not all claims for indemnities or personal injuries have been barred by this policy rationale. There is difficulty, therefore, in defining the limits of this policy in its application to tort cases generally, particularly to those involving personal injury.

4.39 If a wide interpretation is given to the meaning of "benefit" or "profit", so as to include compensation and indemnity, then the principle can be used to explain a

---

[52] We referred to the use of this policy in a criminal law context, such as in the making of confiscation orders under the Drug Trafficking Act 1994. See Consultation Paper No 154 para 6.7 n 10.

[53] Consultation Paper No 154, para 6.8.

[54] See, eg, the comments of Denning J in *Askey v Golden Wine Co Ltd* [1948] 2 All ER 35, 38, quoted above, para 2.21.

[55] See, eg, *Beresford v Royal Insurance Co Ltd* [1938] AC 586. See above, para 2.19.

[56] [1986] 1 All ER 676.

[57] *Ibid*, at p 689.

considerable number of the decisions in which the illegality defence succeeded. However, we do not think the principle works in this way: not all claims which would fall within such a definition have been disallowed.

4.40 Moreover, the application of this concept to tort cases has been the subject of academic[58] and judicial criticism, with the case being argued that in most tort cases the claimant is seeking *compensation* for another's wrongful act rather than a profit or benefit. In *Revill v Newbery*[59] Evans LJ drew the distinction in the following terms:

> [I]t is one thing to deny a plaintiff any fruits from his illegal conduct, but different and more far-reaching to deprive him even of compensation for injury which he suffers and which otherwise he is entitled to recover at law.[60]

4.41 If this viewpoint is correct, cases such as *Cross v Kirkby*[61] and possibly *Clunis v Camden and Islington Health Authority*[62] and *Worrall v British Railways Board*[63] cannot be explained on the basis of the application of the "no profit from own wrongdoing" policy rationale.

4.42 As we noted above, preventing a claimant from profiting can provide the basis behind some of the tort decisions, but we also noted in Part II that the basis for a number of cases seems to be that the claimant cannot rely on his own illegal act as giving rise to a claim. In many of these cases the claimant is not seeking "profit" in the narrower sense that we have discussed: the claim is often for compensation for imprisonment or detention, or loss of employment, as the result of the crime,[64] or an indemnity is being sought for his or her own liability to a third party.[65]

4.43 As these cases do not fall within the "denying profit" policy rationale unless a very wide interpretation is given to "profit" or "benefit", we considered whether there was an argument for saying that the way this policy is stated needs to be widened to cover, for example, "compensation for events or indemnity for liabilities arising from a wrongful act", in order to incorporate these cases. We have provisionally rejected the idea. Broadening the policy in such a way would make it difficult to explain why not all claims for compensation or indemnity arising out of

---

[58] See, eg, N Enonchong, *Illegal Transactions* (1998) p 95, and the comments contained in *Clerk and Lindsell on Torts* (18th ed 2000) para 3-11 n 48.

[59] [1996] QB 567. See above, paras 2.49-2.52.

[60] *Ibid*, at p 579. See also the comments of McLachlin J in *Hall v Hebert* [1993] 2 SCR 159, 176 quoted above, para 3.35.

[61] *The Times* 5 April 2000.

[62] [1998] QB 978.

[63] (Unreported) 29 April 1999.

[64] See, eg, *Clunis v Camden and Islington Health Authority* [1998] QB 978 and *Worrall v British Railways Board* (unreported) 29 April 1999. See above, paras 2.7 and 2.15 n 44.

[65] See, eg, *Meah v McCreamer and others (No 2)* [1986] 1 All ER 943. See above, para 2.8.

involvement in illegal activity are disallowed.[66] It might be possible to explain these cases on the basis of the absence of a close causal link between the illegal act and the injury or loss, but if this has to be done the "no benefit or indemnity" rationale itself loses explanatory power. In any event such an explanation would be inconsistent with those cases where there seems to be a close connection between the claimant's serious illegality and the claim, yet the claim is allowed because technically the claimant does not need to rely on the illegality.[67]

4.44 We think, therefore, that if cases denying compensation or indemnity are to be justifiable, there must be some other policy rationale underlying the illegality doctrine in tort beyond those considered in Consultation Paper No 154 in relation to contract and trusts.

4.45 At the consultation seminar it was suggested that it might be possible to justify the decision to refuse the claim in the cases where compensation for imprisonment or an indemnity for damages paid out was sought, on the ground that the kind of harm suffered by the claimant (or some aspect of it) was not a form of damage for which it was accepted by the law that compensation was payable. This is presumably based on an argument that there is no duty to prevent loss of this nature.[68] We think that the denial of compensation for imprisonment of indemnity is justifiable, but we provisionally think that there are difficulties in accepting this to be on a 'no duty' basis.

4.46 This proposal would only explain a few of the tort cases. In addition, its scope is uncertain. We do not think, for example, that it would apply in the case of a claimant who had been fined (rather than imprisoned) for the breach of a strict liability offence, where there was no question of intent or deliberate fault on the part of the claimant.[69] Perhaps most importantly, this proposal does not in itself help to explain *why* the claim should be barred. An explanation of why claims for compensation for imprisonment or an indemnity should be prevented comes, we think, from the other rationales that we identify in this Part.

4.47 **Our provisional view is that in most tort cases the rationale of preventing a claimant profiting from his or her own wrongdoing will not justify the application of the illegality doctrine, and in particular it will not provide a justification for applying the doctrine in cases where the claim is one for**

---

[66] The plaintiff in *Revill v Newbery* [1996] QB 567 was permitted to recover, despite his attempt to burgle the shed, as were the plaintiffs in *Saunders v Edwards* [1987] 1 WLR 1116, despite their attempt to defraud the Revenue. See above, paras 2.9 and 2.49-2.52.

[67] See, eg, *Webb v Chief Constable of Merseyside Police* [2000] QB 427, where the plaintiffs successfully sued in conversion for the return of money alleged to be the proceeds of drug trafficking. See above, para 2.14.

[68] In the same way that other types of loss are not recognised as being recoverable, eg, mere grief or emotional distress.

[69] Would it be fair to have the same policy operating to deny damages both to an imprisoned rapist and to someone who was fined a small amount for a minor breach of a strict liability regulatory offence? We doubt it: the seriousness of the offence and the state of mind of the offender are things that seem to be taken into account in the current law, and we think they should continue to be taken into account.

compensation arising out of personal injury. We ask whether consultees agree with our provisional views, and if they do not, we ask them to explain why.

(5) Not condoning the illegal activity or encouraging others

4.48 We noted in Part II that a number of judges have referred to the need to ensure that the appearance was not given of condoning the claimant's illegal conduct, or encouraging or assisting the claimant in it.[70] We said earlier in this Part that we are not clear whether this is to be seen as an aspect of the deterrence policy or something separate.[71] In so far as what is meant is that the court should not allow a claim if this would encourage the claimant or others, then it is a policy of deterrence and is subject to our general hesitation to believe that the defence of illegality has much impact on behaviour save in exceptional circumstances.

4.49 However, we are not at all sure that "appearing to condone"[72] should be regarded as simply the word "encouragement" in another form. If this had been the case, it would have been easy enough for the courts to make this clear. Instead, the phrase "not condoning" is regularly repeated. We think there is a case for treating this as a separate policy, based on the *appearance* that the court might create of condoning illegal behaviour of the type engaged in by the claimant, or perhaps creating the appearance of encouraging it, rather than actually encouraging it.

4.50 The rationale of not appearing to assist or encourage the claimant or others seems first to have appeared in the context of the "public conscience" test. It will be recalled that in *Euro-Diam Ltd v Bathurst*[73] Kerr LJ explained that test as follows:

> The *ex turpi causa* defence ultimately rests on a principle of public policy that the courts will not assist a plaintiff who has been guilty of illegal (or immoral) conduct of which the courts should take notice. It applies if in all the circumstances it would be an affront to the public conscience to grant the plaintiff the relief which he seeks because the court would thereby appear to assist or encourage the plaintiff in his illegal conduct or to encourage others in similar acts... .[74]

4.51 Effectively, "no condonation" is a similar rationale but without the reference to the element of "public conscience" excoriated by the House of Lords in *Tinsley v Milligan*.[75] But to the extent that the "no condonation" rationale rests on whether the public would actually perceive the court to be condoning the claimant's

---

[70] See above, paras 2.63-2.67.

[71] See above, para 4.34.

[72] See above, paras 2.65-2.66.

[73] [1990] 1 QB 1.

[74] *Ibid*, at p 35. His was the only full judgment.

[75] [1994] 1 AC 340. See above, paras 2.31-2.42.

conduct, it seems to us to be open to the same objection of being "imponderable" as the "public conscience" test.[76]

4.52 It is possible that the "appearance of condoning" is not meant even in this sense but rather in the sense that it may appear to the court itself that it will be condoning the illegal conduct if it allows the claim. But it is not clear why the appearance to the court itself should matter. If this is the meaning, we feel that the point can be better explained in a different way, by saying that the court should not allow a claim which it thinks to be inconsistent with other rules of the law.

4.53 The other difficulty we have with the "appearance of condoning" rationale is that we are not sure that it in fact offers any very clear guide to decision-making. Does it offer an explanation, for instance, of why the defendant in *Cross v Kirkby*[77] should be able to raise the defence against his attacker, but a motorist who is injured in an accident caused partly by the defendant's negligence and partly by his own reckless driving should not? It is not evident to us that it does, though we would welcome the views of consultees on this issue.

4.54 **It is our provisional view is that a rationale based on "not condoning the illegal activity or appearing to condone or encourage others" does not provide a satisfactory justification for the illegality doctrine in tort. We ask whether consultees agree with our provisional view, and if they do not, we ask them to explain why.**

4.55 We also think that a clearer rationale - though not necessarily one that will always lead to the same answer - to these questions may be provided by the notion of "consistency". This is the argument to which we now turn, though since the argument is a relatively new one[78] for English law (though not for Canadian law[79]) we explain how we have arrived at considering that it may be a more useful rationale than the others so far considered.

(6) "Consistency"

(i) Furthering the purpose of the rule

4.56 We think that it is once again helpful to start with the contract cases. A test which is frequently asked in cases of alleged statutory illegality is whether to refuse the claim would further the purpose of the statute.[80] In the consultation paper we did not treat this as a rationale, but we provisionally proposed that "whether denying relief will further the purpose of the rule which renders the contract illegal" should be one of the factors the court should take into account in exercising its

---

[76] See the speech of Lord Browne-Wilkinson in *Tinsley v Milligan, ibid,* at p 369 and the remarks of Buxton LJ in *Reeves v Commissioner of Police of the Metropolis* [1999] QB 169, 185. See above, paras 2.38-2.39.

[77] *The Times* 5 April 2000. See above, para 2.5.

[78] See below, paras 4.64-4.68.

[79] See above, paras 3.28-3.47.

[80] See Consultation Paper No 154, paras 7.39.

discretion to enforce the contract, or, if it has held the contract to be unenforceable, to allow restitution.[81] Some consultees thought that this should be a prominent[82] factor in any contractual or trusts discretion (one thought it was more in the nature of an overriding principle than an individual factor), although it was remarked that the purpose of a statute was not always easy to determine.

4.57   Having originally suggested that this should be a factor structuring a discretion, we now think that not only is it relevant in this context, but that it forms - or is part of - a further rationale that would go to justify the illegality doctrine on policy grounds. We consider that the illegality doctrine should operate in a way which supports the purpose of the rule which makes the conduct illegal in the first place. Conversely, if allowing the claim would not in any way undermine the purpose of the rule which made the conduct illegal, this rationale will not support the application of the doctrine.

4.58   We believe that a recognition of this concept would go some way to explaining a number of the reported cases. In particular, it helps to explain those cases in which the claimant has tried to recover damages in tort for the fact that he or she has been imprisoned,[83] made the subject of a hospital order,[84] or lost employment and pension rights as a direct result of conviction of a criminal offence.[85] In other cases, an offender might have a fine imposed on him or her, or have to pay compensation[86] to the victims of the crime, and then seek to recover that amount in damages from the defendant. In most of these instances, the courts have invoked the illegality doctrine to prevent the claimant succeeding. We think that, generally, they were right to do so: it would not further the law under which the claimant was punished if he or she were to be compensated for the imprisonment or indemnified for the fine.

4.59   **We ask consultees whether they agree with our provisional view that the concept of "furthering the purpose of the rule" is an important one in providing a justification for the application of the illegality doctrine in tort cases.**

(ii) Consistency

4.60   However, we are attracted to the similar, but broader, policy rationale noted in the Canadian cases by Taylor J in *Mack v Enns*,[87] Sopinka J in *Norberg v Wynrib*,[88] and

---

[81]   Consultation Paper No 154, paras 7.39-7.40.

[82]   One consultee referred to this being a prominent factor in many continental legal systems: see, eg, H Kötz, *European Contract Law* (1997) vol 1, p 162, and K Zweigert and H Kötz, *Introduction to Comparative Law* (3rd ed 1998) pp 386-387.

[83]   We have noted that we think the decision in *Meah v McCreamer* [1985] 1 All ER 367 is wrong. See above, para 2.6.

[84]   See, eg, *Clunis v Camden and Islington Health Authority* [1998] QB 978. See above, para 2.15.

[85]   See, eg, *Worrall v British Railways Board* (unreported) 29 April 1999. See above, para 2.15 n 44.

[86]   See, eg, *Askey v GoldenWine Co Ltd* [1948] 2 All ER 35. See above, para 2.21.

[87]   (1981) 30 BCLR 337, 345.

developed in the decision of the Supreme Court, *Hall v Hebert,*[89] by the majority judgement of McLachlin, La Forest, L'Heureux-Dubé and Iacobucci JJ. This is the notion of preserving the integrity of the legal system through the prevention of internal inconsistency.

4.61 In a narrow sense the requirement of consistency almost certainly exists already in English law. If a claimant was barred from recovering damages in contract, for example, due to the operation of the illegality principle, we think it unlikely that the courts would allow him or her to recover precisely the same amount by way of an action in tort.[90] Certainly we envisaged that under the reforms provisionally proposed in the consultation paper the court would exercise its discretion in this way. We said:

> Where, however, the success of a tortious claim depends on, or is concerned with, a transaction, and that transaction is an "illegal transaction" to which our provisional proposals would apply, we anticipate that the courts would take into account the effect of our provisional proposals on the transaction so as to ensure that the effect of illegality on the tortious claim does not produce an inconsistent result.[91]

4.62 McLachlin J is using "consistency" in a broader sense than this. The judge gave as an example of inconsistency the case of the claimant who seeks an indemnity for a fine imposed on him for his illegal conduct. She said:

> While this example [the claim for a fine] cannot be explained in terms of profit, since the claim is one of compensation for a fine incurred, it does accord with what I have called the more fundamental rationale for the defence of *ex turpi causa,* that based on the need to maintain internal consistency in the law, in the interest of promoting the integrity of the justice system. Again we have a situation where permitting recovery in tort would amount to the law's giving with one hand what it takes away with the other.[92]

4.63 It seems to us that the rationale that can be seen to emerge from the judge's words could explain and justify the use of the illegality doctrine in many of the cases in England and Wales, although it has not generally been clearly articulated in the

---

[88] [1992] SCR 226, 316.

[89] [1993] 2 SCR 159, especially at 179-180. See above, paras 3.28-3.47.

[90] It was suggested by one of the consultation seminar participants that there might be a parallel with the situation of minors' contracts. It seems to be the law that a minor is not liable for a tort which is founded on a contract on which he or she cannot be sued: *Manby v Scott* (1663) 1 Sid 109, 129; *Jennings v Rundall* (1799) 8 Term Rep 335, 336; *Cowern v Neild* [1912] 2 KB 419; and, generally, Halsbury's Laws, vol 5(2), para 627. The minor is liable where the tort, although connected with the contract, is a separate or unconnected act entirely inconsistent with the contract or uncontemplated by it, or if the action in substance arises from the tort itself: *Burnard v Haggis* (1863) 14 CBNS 45; *Walley v Holt* (1876) 35 LT 631; *Fawcett v Smethurst* (1914) 84 LJKB 473; *Ballett v Mingay* [1943] KB 281.

[91] Consultation Paper No 154, para 1.3.

[92] [1993] 2 SCR 159, 178.

case law. We refer to this policy as the need for consistency. A consistent system of law should, we believe, be an aim of any system of justice that seeks to be as fair, as clear and as simple as possible.

4.64 We recognise that the concept of "consistency" may appear to be a new one. However, although the label may seem alien, we think the operation of the concept is not as novel as may first be thought. We think it was at work when Denning J said in *Askey v Golden Wine Co Ltd*:[93]

> [a]ll these objects [the reasons behind the criminal punishment] would be nullified if the offender could recover the amount of the fine and costs from another by process of the civil courts.

4.65 In relation to the law of restitution a similar concept - one termed "stultification" - has been advanced. Writing in *English Private Law*[94] Professor Peter Birks and Dr Peter Marshall, discussing unjust enrichment, explain certain defences (including illegality)[95] as:

> [asserting] that the law would be made ridiculous if the claim in unjust enrichment were allowed. It would be indefensibly conceding with the right hand something which it was endeavouring to prevent with the left.[96]

4.66 They go on to discuss the claim for unjust enrichment by someone who has transferred value under an illegal contract:

> The question then arises whether allowing that claim would make nonsense of the law's refusal to enforce the contract. If it would, the action in unjust enrichment will be barred. It is a separate question whether the claim in unjust enrichment is independently obstructed by grave turpitude.[97]

> The law is nowadays more easily explained by stultification than by turpitude. The reason is that, even up to and including crimes of dishonesty, the courts no longer react to illegality with the decisive revulsion which they once were wont to show. No formal explanation of the results can conceal this truth in cases in which people bent on

---

[93] [1948] 2 All ER 35, 38.

[94] P Birks (ed), *English Private Law* (2000).

[95] Stultification is also used as a rationale operating in relation to bona fide purchase and some other causes of contractual invalidity (apart from illegality).

[96] P Birks (ed), *English Private Law* (2000) vol 2, para 15.290.

[97] Under the rationale of stultification, the illegality defence prevents the claim because of the need to avoid making nonsense of the law's refusal to enforce the contract. This is distinct from using the claimant's turpitude as a reason for barring the claim - that can also occur (presumably under the rules relating to illegality) and can be considered once it is decided that the law would not be stultified by the claim. See *ibid*, at para 15.311.

defrauding the social security system or deceiving their creditors have been allowed to recover.[98]

4.67 Birks and Marshall then use the example of *Parkinson v College of Ambulance Ltd and Harrison*[99] as an example of stultification:

> C pays D money for an honour, and no honour is forthcoming. There is a failure of consideration, but C will be defeated. It suffices to say, without entering into judgments on turpitude, that recovery of the money would stultify the invalidity of the contract. It would provide both a lever to compel performance and a safety net against the event of non-performance, reducing the risks of entering the illegal contract.[100]

It is then pointed out that there would be no stultification if restitution would assist the underlying policy, or where mistake concealed the illegality, or oppression compelled it, or where denial of restitution would entail some greater evil.[101]

4.68 Thus it seems that a similar concept to "consistency" has already been advanced in English law to provide an rationale for the operation of illegality in the area of unjust enrichment. In relation to tort law, as we have said in the above sections, not all the cases can be explained on the basis of the more traditionally articulated policies, and we feel that there must be some other policy that would provide an explanation. We think that the concept of consistency has considerable explanatory power. [102]

---

[98] *Ibid*, at para 15.295-15.296 (footnotes omitted).

[99] [1925] 2 KB 1. See Consultation Paper No 154, para 2.35.

[100] Peter Birks (ed), *English Private Law* (2000) vol 2, para 15.297 (footnote omitted).

[101] This latter result is explained, *ibid*, at para 15.301:

> Stultification is unexplained contradiction. The greater evil which is avoided provides the explanation.

[102] In *Clerk and Lindsell on Torts* (18th ed 2000) para 3-11 n 48 it is suggested that this approach leaves unanswered the questions:

> for whom the courts are seeking to preserve the integrity of the legal system and what does 'integrity' entail?

The answer to the first point may well be that it is for the benefit of society as a whole that the law is seen to have integrity. The second point is perhaps arguable: we would argue it from the point of view of consistency expressed in the body of this section. In addition, the assertion is there made that it is:

> highly unlikely that, say, members of the general public would appreciate the difference between 'compensation' and 'profit' in an award of damages, and moreover would probably have even greater difficulty with the notion that a legal system can retain its 'integrity' whilst at one and the same time prosecuting the burglar for his criminal activity yet requiring the householder to compensate that same burglar for his injuries.

Whilst awards to those acting illegally have drawn criticism from some (particularly sections of the media) in the past, we do not agree with the sweeping and general nature of the above comments.

4.69 Apart from dealing with the difficult issues referred to by McLachlin J, the rationale seems to us to explain a number of apparently technical (and sometimes doubtful) rules. When we considered the *Bowmakers*[103] principle in Part II of this paper, we noted the following possible exceptions to it:

(1) there is an apparent exception for property which it would be illegal for the claimant to possess,[104]

(2) there may also be an exception where to order the return of property would enable the claimant to complete his or her crime,[105] and

(3) there may also be one where it would assist or encourage the claimant or others in criminal acts, as part of the aspect of the general residual test noted in Part II.[106]

It seems to us that the justification for most of these exceptions can be explained by the policy of consistency (the "encouragement" point appears to be a question of deterrence).

4.70 The policy of not allowing someone to profit or benefit from their own wrongdoing may also be seen as an example of the wider need for the law to maintain consistency. It can be argued that it would be inconsistent for the law to proscribe certain forms of conduct on the one hand but to allow someone who has committed such wrongdoing to benefit from it. This appears to us to be a parallel case to that of allowing a claimant to recover compensation for the consequences to himself or herself of his or her criminal act. Just as a person is not allowed to claim to recover the damage arising out of the criminal act that resulted in conviction and sentence, so he or she is not allowed to take any benefit from that wrongdoing. To hold otherwise would mean that in the one case the law would be giving with one hand what it takes with another, in the other case it would be allowing crime to pay. Neither would promote "consistency" in the law.

4.71 In other words, we suggest that the concept of consistency of the legal system may underlie many of the existing rules of illegality in tort, and provide a useful rationale by which to explain many of the cases.

4.72 We are not inclined to go as far as McLachlin J seems to, and assert that this is the *only* valid rationale for the doctrine of illegality. We suggest the concepts of "dignity", "deterrence" and "no benefit" are also valid. However, given the very limited occasions when these other rationales are likely to be applicable in a tort case, the concept of consistency seems to us a useful one in explaining many of the tort cases on a justifiable policy basis.

---

[103] *Bowmakers Ltd v Barnet Instruments Ltd* [1945] KB 65. See above, para 2.13.

[104] See above, para 2.17.

[105] See above, para 2.18.

[106] See above, paras 2.63-2.67.

4.73 In Part VI we suggest that, were the court to be given a statutory discretion whether to allow the defence of illegality on the ground that the claim arose out of, or is connected to, an illegal act on the claimant's part, the concept of consistency could be a useful one in deciding whether to invoke the doctrine of illegality. If to allow a claim can be shown to result in inconsistency - such as in *Clunis v Camden and Islington Health Authority*[107] or *Worrall v British Railways Board*[108] - then there is justification for barring the claim. However, if to allow the claim would not be inconsistent, then we think that to apply the illegality doctrine in the circumstances of most tort cases would be unjustified.

4.74 When we discussed the concept of consistency at the consultation seminar it received a mixed reception with some strongly expressed views: some agreed strongly with us that its explanatory power was helpful, whilst others were not in favour of it. What troubles us is that if it is not an acceptable rationale (either on the basis of the narrower "purpose of the statute" approach or the wider "integrity of the legal system" approach) then many of the reported cases that apply the current rules of the doctrine seem to have no underlying justification. When we are concerned with the draconian effects of the illegality doctrine, this does not seem fair or just. To reach such a conclusion would lead us to a number of stark possibilities:

(1) as an unjustifiable doctrine, we should recommend its total abolition in tort, or alternatively its partial abolition save in those very rare situations when it can be justified on the more limited "traditional" rationales, or

(2) we accept as a given that there is no real justification for many of the cases, and wait for this fact either to be recognised or ignored by the courts in this country or in Strasbourg, or

(3) there is another rationale or interpretation that we have not considered that would explain most of the tort cases.

(7) "Responsibility"

4.75 On the question of whether there is any other rationale, it was suggested at the consultation seminar that one might be provided by the concept of "responsibility". It was argued that in law everyone is to be treated as being responsible for their own acts and the reasonably foreseeable consequences of those acts for themselves and for others: in other words, there would be no duty owed by another because the claimant must be responsible for his or her own actions. If a person committed an unlawful act and suffered because of it, then he or she should not be awarded compensation for it. Thus, it was argued, the burglar who is bitten by the householder's dog should not have a claim.

4.76 We are not convinced that this provides an adequate rationale for the defence of illegality. It seems more appropriate as a justification of the defence of assumption

---

[107] [1998] QB 978.

[108] (Unreported) 29 April 1999.

of risk (*volenti non fit injuria*) than of the defence of illegality. If a claimant has deliberately put himself or herself in the way of harm, it is this willing acceptance of risk that will result in the claimant being held to have accepted the risk of injury. It is quite true, as we indeed argue in the next section,[109] that many of the "illegality" cases can be explained in this way - for example, the safe blowers who take a high risk in the way they use explosives and blow themselves up can be said to accept the risk of injury just as much as the shotfirers who test a detonator without proper precautions.[110] But we do not think that in every case in which illegality might be held to bar the claim it can be said that the claimant had accepted responsibility for his or her injury in any real sense. The criminal who seeks to recover the profits of his or her crime from a co-conspirator probably gave no thought to the risk of being cheated by the latter.

4.77   It might be argued that the question is not whether the criminal genuinely accepted responsibility for his or her own injury, but that he or she should be treated as doing so. But then this approach ceases to explain why the criminal must be treated in this way. Nor does it help to draw the boundaries. For example, it does not help to explain why it is that a burglar who has been savaged by the defendant's dog should not (we will assume) recover, but a trespasser without burglarious intent who was so injured should be able to recover. Both are trespassers and have deliberately chosen to go where they should not be, and have suffered as a result of their actions. Yet few people, we suspect, would wish mere trespassers to be subject to the illegality defence.[111]

4.78   It might also be argued that the "responsibility" rationale is not aimed at defences; the point being that there simply should be no duty owed to such a person. But we consider that an approach that results in there being no duty is open to the criticisms noted in *Hall v Hebert*.[112] Shifting the analysis to a question of duty provides no new insight into the fundamental question of when the courts should deny recovery in tort on the ground of the claimant's illegal conduct. Nor does it provide any further help in distinguishing between cases such as those of the burglar and the mere trespasser.

4.79   It was also suggested at the consultation seminar that the 'no duty' approach would deal with situations where it could be argued to be odd that the law would recognise duties as between persons. The example was given of bank robbers. Was the person who masterminded the plan to rob a bank to owe the normal employer's duty of providing a safe system of work? We think that this rather colourful example masks what we think are the realities of the situation. Such a situation would be likely to be met with the defence of assumption of risk. To take a more realistic situation, suppose a building site owner employed workers in circumstances of illegality (for example, because there was an attempt to defraud

---

[109]   See below, para 4.91.

[110]   See *Imperial Chemical Industries Ltd v Shatwell* [1965] AC 656.

[111]   A point that must have been recognised by Parliament, given the existence of the Occupier's Liability Act 1984. See above, para 2.50.

[112]   [1993] 2 SCR 159, 181-185. See above, paras 3.36-3.39.

the Revenue by not paying tax or National Insurance, or the workers did not have the required work permits). Should the court say there was no duty of care owed in these circumstances? We do not think so. Where should the line be drawn, for the purposes of establishing a duty, between people who seek to defraud the Revenue and people who seek to rob banks? It is not possible to draw up a finite list of situations. We think there must be a line between conduct that will affect a claim and conduct that will not, but we think the better approach would be to hold that whatever duty might theoretically arise in the case of the bank robber, the discretion that we propose later in this consultation paper would operate so as to prevent the claim.[113] In any event, the extreme cases are likely to be met with a claim of assumption of risk, or the circumstances will be such that the court cannot find a duty in the normal way ("cannot" rather than "will not").[114]

4.80   **Our provisional view, therefore, is that the concept of "taking responsibility for one's own actions" does not provide a satisfactory rationale for the existence of the illegality doctrine. However, we would welcome the views of consultees on this proposed rationale.**

4.81   **Thus it is our provisional view that**

(1)   **to justify the tort cases it is necessary to develop some further rationale beyond "dignity", "deterrence", "no profit", "no condonation" and "responsibility"; and**

(2)   **the best new rationale is that expressed by McLachlin J in *Hall v Hebert*, the need to maintain consistency in the law.**

We ask consultees whether they agree with this view, and if not, what they regard as valid justifications for the existence of the doctrine in tort.

(8) Particular cases

(i) Injuries suffered in the course of illegal activity

4.82   In our review of the illegality defence in tort cases, one of the issues that has concerned us is the rationale of allowing the illegality defence to prevent someone who has been injured through the negligence or other fault of the defendant from claiming damages on the ground that the claimant was engaged in some illegal activity. Although it is certainly not every illegal activity which will lead to this result, we have seen several cases of this type in which it has been held that the defendant could use the illegality defence. Our difficulty has been to reconcile these cases - or rather, the use of the illegality defence in these cases[115] - with the rationales we have identified for the illegality defence in tort.

---

[113] See below, Part VI.

[114] See below, paras 4.88-4.90.

[115] We think each case which might be criticised on this ground can be justified on some other basis, frequently one on which the court also relied as an alternative ground. Thus our

84

4.83 We have provisionally rejected the rationale of "punishment".[116] We have explained that, like several judges both in England and the Commonwealth, we not do think these cases fit within the "no benefit" rationale.[117] We have expressed reservations about the rationales of "dignity" and "deterrence" save in exceptional cases [118] and we have doubted the strength or usefulness of the "no condonation" argument.[119] We have also doubted a rationale based on "responsibility".[120] What rationale does underlie these cases?

4.84 Can these cases be justified on the basis that to allow recovery would tend to undermine the rule making the activity illegal? Or, to use the approach of the Canadian Supreme Court, would it render the law inconsistent? Unless one of these rationales applies, or there is some further rationale which we have failed to identify, it seems to mean that the illegality defence should not be applied, or at least be applied only in very exceptional circumstances, in "personal injury" cases.

4.85 It was precisely this question which the Supreme Court of Canada was addressing in *Hall v Hebert*,[121] and which McLachlin J used the consistency argument to answer. She said:

> The power [to deny recovery to a plaintiff on the ground that to do so would undermine the integrity of the justice system] is a limited one...Its use is not justified where the plaintiff's claim is merely for compensation for personal injuries sustained as a consequence of the negligence of the defendant.[122]

4.86 We too doubt whether it is "inconsistent" to allow a claim for personal injury caused by the default of the defendant where the claimant was engaging in illegal or criminal activity at the time he or she was injured.

4.87 This does not mean that we think the outcomes of the decided English cases were incorrect. In our view the cases were quite correctly decided on other grounds. Thus we think that both *Ashton v Turner*[123] and *Pitts v Hunt*[124] were cases in which the claims should fail but on the ground of lack of duty rather than of illegality.

concern is with the way in which the illegality defence has been stated rather than with the outcomes of the English cases to date.

[116] See above, paras 4.10-4.24.

[117] See above, paras 4.39-4.41.

[118] See above, paras 4.26 and 4.31-4.33.

[119] See above, paras 4.51-4.53.

[120] See above, paras 4.75-4.80.

[121] [1993] 2 SCR 159.

[122] *Ibid*, at pp 179-180.

[123] [1981] 1 QB 137. See above, para 2.27.

[124] [1991] 1 QB 24. See above, para 2.4.

4.88   *Pitts v Hunt*[125] can be seen as a case of the driver being encouraged by the passenger to drive in the manner that ultimately led to the passenger being injured. It does not lie easily in the mouth of the passenger to claim that a duty was owed to him by the driver not to drive in the very way that the passenger was encouraging.[126] Thus on the particular facts of this case there is a strong argument for saying that there was no duty. *Ashton v Turner*[127] may also be explicable on a similar basis: the driver was driving in the manner encouraged by the passenger, so as to escape pursuit following a burglary. It can be argued that where the passenger expressly or implicitly asked the driver to drive in a particular way, a duty not to drive in that way does not arise.

4.89   It can even be said that in cases such as those mentioned above, the fact that the plaintiff was acting illegally has little to do with the denial of duty. There is no duty because of the particular individual facts of the case; that those circumstances were ones of illegality is incidental. We think it would be arguable that there would be no duty on facts like those in *Pitts v Hunt* even if the parties had been driving on a private road and not trying to frighten anyone, so that their conduct was not illegal. It could be said that the fact that the plaintiff was encouraging the driver to swerve and to weave about would make it impossible to say that the defendant was under a duty to the plaintiff not to drive in this dangerous manner.

4.90   The English cases involving driving where it has been held that there was no duty are therefore explicable without illegality being an essential part of the decision. Because of the factual circumstances, a duty *cannot* be found. We contrast this approach with that taken by some of the Australian cases, where a duty has been denied as a matter of policy - in other words, where a duty *will not* be found.[128]

4.91   In some cases an alternative analysis would be that the claimant had accepted the risk of injury. In *Pitts v Hunt*[129] it was held that the defence of *volenti non fit injuria* is not available in those cases arising out of negligent driving,[130] because of what is now sections 149(2) and (3) of the Road Traffic Act 1988.[131] This does not apply to the oft-cited example of two people trying to break into a safe using explosives and one injuring the other.

---

[125]   *Ibid.*

[126]   Against this it has been argued that these sorts of cases should be approached on the basis that, as a user of the highway, the driver owes the passenger a duty to drive with reasonable care and skill despite the encouragement or instructions of the passenger. See the discussion on this point in *Clerk and Lindsell on Torts* (18th ed 2000) para 3-05.

[127]   [1981] QB 137.

[128]   See above, paras 3.2-3.27.

[129]   [1991] 1 QB 24.

[130]   Holding that Ewbank J was wrong to hold that it was an available defence in *Ashton v Turner* [1981] QB 137.

[131]   Then s 148(3) of the Road Traffic Act 1972.

4.92 Both *Ashton v Turner* and *Pitts v Hunt* are different to the case where the passenger has not suggested or encouraged the course of action actually taken by the driver. If the passenger in *Ashton v Turner* had been injured later in the journey home, rather than in the course of the get-away, we think that he should have been owed a duty of care by the driver; and it follows from what we said earlier that we are not convinced that there is any valid rationale for barring his claim on the ground of illegality.[132]

4.93 Similarly, we do not doubt the actual outcome of *Cross v Kirkby*.[133] It will be recalled that the claimant was seeking damages for personal injury he had sustained following his own attack on the defendant. The claim failed for two reasons: the defendant had used no more force than was reasonable in self-defence, and the claim was so closely linked to the claimant's unlawful conduct that it should fail. We have no difficulty with the first ground, but, in the light of our review of the rationales for the illegality, we are unclear on what policy basis the decision on the illegality point is justifiable.

4.94 Our concern - to which we will return in Part V of this paper - is that a subsequent court might take the statement of the illegality rule in *Cross v Kirkby* and similar cases and apply it without considering whether the rationales really justify the decision. For example, had it been held that the defendant had used more force than was reasonable in self-defence, would the claim still have been rejected on the grounds of illegality?

4.95 Such an outcome is far from certain. A court faced with this situation might well hold that, because the blow struck by the defendant was excessive, the injury suffered as a result was not "closely connected" to his own criminal conduct in assaulting the defendant. It would certainly be open to a court to decide the case in this way. However, we think it quite possible that the illegality defence stated by Beldam LJ -

> the principle applies when the claimant's claim is so closely connected or inextricably bound up with his own criminal or illegal activity that the court could not permit him to recover without appearing to condone that conduct[134]

- might be applied even when the defendant was not acting reasonably in self-defence. Equally, it might be applied to bar the claim of one joy-rider against another even though they were not deliberately engaging in dangerous driving or attempting a get-away, but, for instance, simply driving home.[135]

---

[132] We would not follow the decision in the Australian case of *Godbolt v Fittock* [1963] SR (NSW) 617. See above, para 3.6.

[133] *The Times* 5th April 2000. See above, para 2.5.

[134] *Per* Beldam LJ *ibid* (Smith Bernal transcript).

[135] A claim was refused in similar circumstances in the Australian case of *Godbolt v Fittock* [1963] SR (NSW) 617, in which cattle rustlers were on their way home when the driver fell asleep at the wheel. See above, para 3.6.

4.96 If this is so, we are not convinced that the outcome could be justified by the rationales we have identified. A number of judges in other jurisdictions[136] have been cautious over the use of the illegality defence in cases involving personal injury, and in this country there are *dicta* which seem to us to hint, at least, at the same feeling.[137] We share these concerns.

4.97 If, on the other hand, the illegality defence would not be applied in these hypothetical cases, we ask whether the defence is needed at all for this type of personal injury case, since it seems to add nothing to the analysis.

4.98 **We invite consultees' views on the questions:**

   (1)   **can the denial of a claim for personal injury caused to the claimant by the defendant's negligence or other wrong while the claimant was engaged in some illegal activity be justified by any of the rationales we have identified?**

   (2)   **If not, are there further rationales by which these cases may be justified?**

(ii) "No reliance" cases

4.99 Conversely, we also have doubts about the rationale behind allowing the claimant to recover, despite a connection between his claim and an illegal act, on the ground that he does not need to rely on the illegal act to make out his claim. It was precisely this approach which was taken in *Tinsley v Milligan*[138] and with which we expressed provisional disagreement in Consultation Paper No 154. We pointed out that the principle seems to operate arbitrarily in so far as the outcome depends on the identity of the transferor and transferee.[139] To apply the same rule in tort cases seems in principle open to the same objection. Certainly the rule does not seem to link the application of the defence to the underlying rationales.

4.100 Again, we are not questioning the outcome of the tort cases decided on this approach. *Clunis v Camden and Islington Health Authority*,[140] for example, seems entirely justifiable if the rationale of consistency is accepted: it would be quite inconsistent to imprison or detain someone on the grounds that he was responsible for a serious offence and then to compensate him for the detention. Conversely, the same rationale may be used (although this may be arguable) to explain why in *Webb v Chief Constable of Merseyside Police*[141] the claimant was permitted to recover the money even though it may have represented the proceeds of drug dealing: there was a statutory scheme for confiscation which did not cover

---

[136] See above, Part III.

[137] See the remark of Evans LJ in *Revill v Newbery* [1996] QB 567, 579, quoted above, para 2.23.

[138] [1994] 1 AC 340.

[139] Consultation Paper No 154, para 3.22.

[140] [1998] QB 978. See above, para 2.7.

[141] [2000] QB 427. See above, para 2.14.

a case in which there had been no conviction and the court was not prepared to make what would amount to an extension of the statutory scheme.

4.101 Moreover, the situation may be less problematic because, as we have pointed out, there are some apparent exceptions under which the claim may be refused.[142] A case under which the claimant does not rely on the illegal act may nevertheless be denied under the residual general principle.

4.102 Nonetheless, it seems to us a general principle to the effect that a claim will not be allowed if the claimant has to rely on his illegal act, and conversely will be disallowed if he need not, is not clearly explicable in terms of the rationales for the illegality defence.

3. CONCLUSION

4.103 Having reappraised the rationales that lie behind the existence of the doctrine of illegality, we maintain our view that its use is still justified in principle in contract and trusts cases, although as we develop our policy in this area we are clear that we need to ensure that our provisional proposals accord with the underlying rationales. We also consider use of the illegality doctrine to be justified in some cases framed in tort, although we suspect that successful invocation of the doctrine in practice, where compensatory damages for personal injury are claimed, may not be that common.

4.104 We have argued that the rationales given for the illegality defence in contract and trusts cases in Consultation Paper No 154 do not adequately justify the tort cases. The denial of a tort claim based solely on the policy of deterrence, or on the need to protect the dignity of the courts, will, we think, very rarely be justifiable. We think there is a need to recognise a further rationale in order for the doctrine to operate generally on a justifiable basis. This might be that the claim should not be allowed if to allow it would undermine the rule making the conduct illegal, or, as we would prefer to put it, would render the law inconsistent. We are very conscious, however, that others may not share our provisional view on this type of case; and indeed, may not find the "consistency" rationale to be persuasive.

4.105 We have raised the question whether the application of the defence is justified in two classes of case, and think the concept of consistency provides a rationale for *not* denying compensation to those who have suffered personal injury, save in very exceptional cases.

4.106 In discussing the concept of consistency, we have said that we think that it has significant explanatory power when considering the tort case law. We have not formed a view as to whether it is a concept that helps to explain the operation of the doctrine in the area of contract and trusts. However, it may be that in contract and trusts the existing rationales work sufficiently well, so that there is less need for any new rationale to explain the cases. We would be interested in consultees'

---

[142] Eg, if the claim is for property which it would be illegal for the claimant to possess, or if to order the return of the property would enable the claimant to complete his crime. See above, paras 2.16-2.18.

views on whether the concept of consistency would encompass any of the rationales as they operate in contract and trusts.[143]

4.107 **We would welcome views on whether the same rationales that we have identified for use of the illegality defence in tort cases apply to contract and trust cases - in particular, whether consultees consider that the "consistency" rationale is a useful one to explain the policy which should underlie the illegality defence in contract and trusts.**

---

[143] Although we noted above that it might be possible to argue that the "no benefit" rationale could be seen as part of a wider consistency rationale. See above, para 4.70.

PART V
THE CASE FOR REFORM

5.1 In Parts II and III of this paper we gave detailed consideration to the operation of the law of illegality in tort, and in Part IV we attempted to identify the rationales underlying the application of the defence. We now turn to the question of whether there is a need for reform in this area.

1. IS AN ILLEGALITY DEFENCE NEEDED IN TORT?

5.2 The first question must be whether there is a need for a doctrine of illegality within tort law at all. If there is no need, then it would seem appropriate to suggest abolition of the doctrine.[1]

5.3 It can be argued that as most of the reported cases where the illegality doctrine has been successful were also decided on other grounds there is no real need to retain the doctrine. Whilst we acknowledge that there is some strength in this point, we do not think it provides a sufficient ground on which to justify abolishing the doctrine. It is not the case that *every* reported decision has been decided on multiple grounds, and it is easy to envisage slight factual differences to the current cases which would result in the illegality point being the decisive issue.[2]

5.4 We think the need for tort law to retain some form of the illegality doctrine is shown by two simple situations. The first is where a claimant might avoid the consequences of the operation of the doctrine as it applies in contract or other areas by suing in tort instead. For example, B enters into an illegal contract with A, relying on A's fraudulent representation (but which representation has nothing to do with the illegal nature of the contract). The court, in exercising its statutory discretion, refuses to enforce the contract because of the illegality or to grant restitution to B, thus leaving B out of pocket. If there were no illegality defence in tort, B might be able to claim damages for fraud on the basis that, had A not made the representation, B would not have entered into the contract. B might then claim damages amounting to an indemnity for all his or her losses,[3] or for the lost opportunity to make some other (legal) arrangement that would have brought a similar financial reward.[4] If such claims could not be disallowed on the basis of

---

[1] This was the course suggested by some of those who attended the consultation seminar or responded to the draft consultation paper.

[2] Such as a finding in the case of *Cross v Kirkby, The Times* 5 April 2000 that the defendant had *not* been acting in self-defence. See above, para 2.5.

[3] Cf *Smith New Court Securities Ltd v Scrimgeour Vickers (Asset Management) Ltd* [1997] AC 254.

[4] Cf *East v Maurer* [1991] 1 WLR 461.

illegality, the effect of the statutory discretion being exercised so as to prevent enforcement of the contract or restitution would be undermined.[5]

5.5 We do not believe claims in tort are entirely fanciful. There are several reported tort cases that arise out of, or are connected to, illegal contracts, including the well-known case of *Taylor v Chester*,[6] in which at least one head of the claim the plaintiff made to recover the half-note he had deposited as security for the payment of his bill in a brothel was in tort.[7]

5.6 The second situation is where a claimant might sue in tort for damages in respect of imprisonment or for the recovery of a fine imposed on him or her, or for the recovery of property that it would be illegal to possess. To allow such claims would, as Denning J pointed out in *Askey v Golden Wine Co Ltd*,[8] undermine other parts of the law. It has been suggested that if the illegality doctrine were abolished then the cases in this second category might be dealt with by using causation: either the illegal conduct of the claimant would break the causal chain, in which case there would be no claim, or it would not, in which case recovery would be permitted (if, for example, the claimant had not been at fault). However, we do not think that this is an adequate basis for abolishing the doctrine. We think the case law demonstrates that there is sufficient strength of feeling amongst some judges that, if illegality were to be abolished as a defence in tort, it would simply reappear in another guise, such as through the manipulation of causation, or, perhaps more likely, as an increase of instances in which it was held that, because the claimant had been acting illegally, there was no duty of care. Such decisions would simply be a mask for the illegality doctrine. We think that this would make the situation worse, rather than better. Thus some defence of illegality is needed, we believe. However, how widely it should be applied is debatable. We go on to consider the limits of the doctrine in this consultation paper.[9]

---

[5] In the recent case of *MacDonald v Myerson and another* [2001] EGCS 15 the claimant had bought two properties by means of a mortgage fraud. Later he instructed the defendant solicitors to sell the properties, which they did (despite being aware of injunctive proceedings to restrain the claimant from dealing with assets that were the subject of the indictment). After the mortgages had been paid off a balance remained with the solicitors but they refused to pay it to the claimant on the basis that it was the proceeds of fraud. The Court of Appeal allowed the claim on the ground that the claimant did not have to rely on the fraud to show his entitlement to the money. Such a case would presumably fall within the statutory discretion which we provisionally proposed in Consultation Paper No 154, and it might be that on these facts a future court would apply the discretion to disallow the claim. However, the case is loosely parallel to that of *Webb v Chief Constable of Merseyside Police* [2000] QB 427 (see above, para 2.14), save that the action in *Webb* was for conversion. It would be odd if that claim was allowed in tort, but a similar one in trusts barred.

[6] (1869) LR 4 QB 309.

[7] See also, eg, *Bowmakers Ltd v Barnet Instruments Ltd* [1945] KB 65, although in that case the claim was allowed. See above, para 2.13.

[8] [1948] 2 All ER 35, 38. See above, para 2.21.

[9] One of the responses we received on the draft of this consultation paper questioned whether it was right that, in a case such as *Thackwell v Barclays Bank Ltd* [1986] 1 All ER 676, the product of a fraud which the illegality doctrine prevented the claimant from taking should remain with the party that has converted it, rather than being confiscated by the State. This

5.7   **We ask consultees whether they agree with our provisional proposal that a defence of illegality in tort in some form should be retained.**

2. REASONS FOR REFORM

5.8   Whilst we believe that a doctrine is needed, we also believe that reform is needed. There are essentially three reasons for reform. These are: (1) the need to avoid different regimes for overlapping or closely related claims; (2) a current lack of clarity, and (3) the potential for inappropriate development under the current system. We consider each of these points in turn.

(1) The need to avoid different regimes for overlapping or closely related claims

5.9   In Consultation Paper No 154 we set out our provisional proposals for reforming the law as it applies to contract and trusts, suggesting the replacement of the current rules with a statutory discretion, structured around a number of factors.[10] We are considering our final policy in this area in the light of the consultation process. However, assuming, as is likely, that our final Report contains a recommendation for legislative reform along the lines provisionally proposed, we think that there is a real risk of confusion in having in operation two different regimes in respect of the same doctrine: a structured statutory discretion for contract and trusts, and an unreformed, common law approach for tort.[11] Having different rules risks not only simple confusion, but also the possibility of inconsistent results.

5.10   In *Saunders v Edwards*,[12] for example, a dispute arose out of the sale of the lease of a flat after the defendant had fraudulently represented that it included a roof garden. The plaintiffs had sought to defraud the Inland Revenue by seeking to avoid paying stamp duty, by understating the true value of the flat. The action was based on the tort of deceit: no action was brought for specific performance of the contract or for damages for breach.[13] What if a similar situation were to arise again but with a contractual claim included in the alternative? If the law on illegality was reformed in respect of contract and trusts, but not tort, the court would be required to apply a legislative, structured discretion when considering the effect of illegality for the contractual aspect of the claim, yet in the same case would have to have regard to the very different common law regime for the tortious aspect, even

---

gives rise to the question whether the court should be given such a power to confiscate. This is a difficult and controversial question but it is outside the terms of reference of this consultation paper. In the absence of such a power of confiscation, where the claim is for the proceeds of a crime we think it would be "inconsistent" to allow recovery of this 'benefit' (see above, para 4.70) even if the defendant's case for retaining the money is weak.

[10]   See Consultation Paper No 154, Parts VII and VIII.

[11]   The operation of two different regimes was one of the reasons that some of those who responded to the consultation paper suggested that we widen the scope of our examination of the effect of illegality to include tort.

[12]   [1987] 1 WLR 1116. See above, para 2.9.

[13]   *Ibid*, at p 1125. In this case the illegality did not operate so as to prevent the plaintiffs' claim.

if the result were the same. Such an approach is likely to give rise to confusion, and we believe that it should be avoided.

5.11 In addition to the risk of confusion, having two different regimes has the potential for inconsistent results, with the tort rules undermining the effect of the statutory discretion for contract. We noted examples of possible claims in tort when we discussed the need for a defence of illegality.[14] It is not inconceivable that under the current doctrine as it applies in tort, one of these claims might be allowed, particularly if B could frame his claim in such a way as to avoid relying on the illegality of the contract. At least in a case like *Taylor v Chester*[15] it is not clear that this would be impossible.

5.12 It is part of the Law Commission's statutory duty to review the law, with a view to its systematic development and reform, including the elimination of anomalies and generally the simplification and modernisation of the law.[16] We think that having a single regime would further these aims.

5.13 **We therefore ask consultees whether they agree with us that there would be a real risk of confusion and inconsistency if the law in relation to contract and trusts were to be reformed by legislation but tort law left unreformed. Do consultees agree with us that this reason is sufficient to put the reform of illegality as it affects tort law on a statutory footing?**

5.14 We also think that it would be a helpful step towards these goals if, ultimately, we were able to develop not just a similar statutory discretion but also a common set of factors to which the court could refer without having to categorise the claim based on often artificial boundaries between, say, contract and tort. We return to this theme later in this paper, but we would be interested to know whether consultees agree with us that this would be desirable.

(2) Lack of clarity

5.15 We have already noted in Part II of this paper that the approach taken by the courts in applying the doctrine to tort actions is unclear and sometimes confusing. It is not possible to discern one standard approach by the courts when they are deciding the impact of the illegality doctrine in a tort case. This makes it difficult to predict the outcome of a case when the court is considering the claimant's illegal conduct. There are several elements that give rise to this lack of clarity.

---

[14] See above, paras 5.4-5.5.

[15] (1869) LR 4 QB 309. See above, para 5.5.

[16] See Law Commissions Act 1965, s 3(1):

> It shall be the duty of [the Law Commission] to take and keep under review all the law with which [it is] concerned with a view to its systematic development and reform, including in particular the codification of such law, the elimination of anomalies, the repeal of obsolete and unnecessary enactments, the reduction of the number of separate enactments and generally the simplification and modernisation of the law... .

(i) The duty of care approach

5.16 We explained in Part II that some of the cases in England and Wales deny that a duty of care exists as between the parties to an illegal joint enterprise. We also noted in Part III that the Australian courts have developed this concept to the extent that the court is more likely to refuse to find a duty as a matter of policy than to apply an illegality defence.

5.17 We accept that there are cases in which a finding that the defendant owed no duty to the claimant is quite proper and indeed inevitable, because the defendant was doing just what the claimant was encouraging him to do.[17] We do not think it helpful to take this approach further and deny a duty on the basis that the claimant's activity was illegal - in other words, to extend it from cases in which a duty *cannot* be found because of the factual circumstances to ones in which a duty *will not* be found because of the illegality. The danger of this approach is that it obscures why the duty is being denied.[18]

5.18 Even if no legislative reform were forthcoming at the conclusion of our examination of the law, we would provisionally recommend that the courts should not approach the question of illegality as one of duty of care, outside the sort of situation such as in *Pitts v Hunt*[19] which can be seen as a case where the illegality is incidental to the denial of duty, rather than a reason for it.

(ii) The "public conscience" test

5.19 As we have seen in Part II of this paper, some of the reasoning expressed in the cases suggests that the court may take a pragmatic view, referring to something similar to the "public conscience" test, despite this concept having been expressly disapproved of and rejected (in the context of trusts law at least) by the House of Lords in *Tinsley v Milligan*.[20] However, not all tort cases use this "public conscience" approach[21] - it seems to be just one of a variety of approaches taken by the court, which adds to the difficulty of predicting how a court will approach a case involving some aspect of illegality.

(iii) Causation or 'direct connection'

5.20 Some of the tort cases seem to have approached the question as a matter of causation or 'closeness of connection'.[22] This may at first seem an attractive way of justifying the result reached in a number of the cases, but we think that there is a problem with this approach. Causation can be a useful mechanism for explaining

---

[17] In several situations the circumstances may be such as to amount to *volenti non fit injuria*.

[18] Cf the approach found in some of the Australian cases. See above, paras 3.2-3.27. See further above, paras 2.30 n 75 and 3.36-3.39 for criticism of the 'no duty' approach.

[19] [1991] 1 QB 24.

[20] [1994] 1 AC 340.

[21] Eg, Beldam LJ referred to the House of Lords' disapproval of the "public conscience" test when giving the judgment of the Court of Appeal in *Clunis v Camden and Islington Health Authority* [1998] QB 978, 989.

[22] See, eg, *Saunders v Edwards* [1987] 1 WLR 1116. See above, paras 2.53-2.55.

a decision after it has been reached, but a difficult one for predicting how a court will decide. The 'close connection' test provides little means of assessing how close the connection has to be.[23]

(iv) Seriousness of illegality

5.21 It seems that the seriousness of the illegal conduct is a factor which features in some of the cases. Whilst we agree that this is an important factor,[24] there is currently no means of assessing how serious the illegality has to be before the illegality rule is invoked, or in which cases seriousness will be considered important.[25]

(v) Vagueness of reasoning

5.22 In several cases is it not clear what justification there is for the doctrine being invoked, and in others the reasoning or approach varies even between members of the same court.[26] Many cases refer to Lord Mansfield's comments in *Holman v Johnson,*[27] and subsequent decisions, but do not go on to explain the rationale for the application of Lord Mansfield's words to the particular case being dealt with. We noted in Part II the difficulties in trying to establish a clear exposition of how the current rules operate in tort.

5.23 In short, we believe that the lack of clarity discussed in the above paragraphs makes it difficult to predict the approach of a court or the outcome of a tort case where the illegality doctrine is invoked, and can lead to perceived or actual arbitrariness. Our provisional conclusion, therefore, is that reform would be advantageous. We believe that the operation of a carefully structured discretion[28] would be more predictable and less arbitrary than the current series of somewhat haphazard rules.

---

[23] Difficulties with explaining the cases in terms purely of causation or closeness of connection have helped lead us to the view that the concept of consistency has significant explanatory power. See above, Part IV.

[24] Our provisional proposals for reform are that it forms one of the factors we suggest the court should take into account. See below, para 6.25.

[25] Cf, eg, *Webb v Chief Constable of Merseyside Police* [2000] QB 427 and *Cross v Kirkby, The Times* 5 April 2000. In the former case, serious illegality (drug dealing) was probably involved (although the claimant was unconvicted), but insufficient to bar the claim as the claimant did not have to rely on that illegality to make his claim. In the latter case, the serious illegality (assault) was not relied on by the claimant, but the claim was still barred by the court. See above, paras 2.5 and 2.14.

[26] See, eg, the judgments of Beldam, Balcombe and Dillon LJJ in *Pitts v Hunt* [1991] 1 QB 24. See above, paras 2.28-2.29.

[27] (1775) 1 Cowp 341; 98 ER 1120. See para 6.2 of Consultation Paper No 154.

[28] See below, Part VI.

(3) Potential for inappropriate development

(i) Personal injury cases

5.24   In Part IV we said that we have some difficulty in seeing the rationale underlying some of the applications of the illegality doctrine, in particular when someone who has been injured through the negligence or other fault of the defendant is prevented from claiming damages on the ground that when they were injured they were engaged in some illegal activity. We said that we accept the outcomes of the cases, in so far as they rest on other grounds, but we were not convinced that application of the illegality defence was justified. Our fear is that the statements of the illegality doctrine in some of these cases may encourage lower courts to deny claims in situations in which we do not think it is justifiable to do so in terms of the rationales for the defence. There is some risk of inappropriate decisions if the law remains unclear and the application of the defence is not carefully limited.

5.25   We have said that we believe that the doctrine of illegality is not one that should be lightly invoked, and that it is important that it should only be used in a way that properly reflects the policy rationales that justify its existence. We think that where a claimant who has acted illegally seeks to sue in tort, the fact that he or she has so acted should only bar the claim on the ground that to hold otherwise would result in the infringement of one or more of those rationales, and then only if such a step was a proportionate one.[29]

5.26   Take, for example, a variant on the facts of *Cross v Kirkby*.[30] We suggested earlier that the outcome of that case was entirely justifiable on the facts, but that if the defendant had used more force than was reasonable it would not necessarily be justifiable, in terms of the rationales we had identified, to refuse the claim. To recap, our provisional view is that it is not necessary to apply the defence in order to deny a profit or a windfall benefit, as the claimant was only seeking compensatory damages; denying compensation in these circumstances is not likely to deter people from carrying out attacks;[31] to allow the claim would not be likely to impugn the dignity of the court;[32] and it would not result in inconsistency with the law which the claimant fell foul of, or allow him to claim damages resulting from his own conviction or punishment.[33]

5.27   Our concern is that a subsequent court might take the statement of the illegality rule in *Cross v Kirkby* and similar cases and apply it without considering whether the rationales really justify its decision. In other words, although we do not believe

---

[29]   See below, para 6.29.

[30]   *The Times* 5th April 2000.

[31]   For deterrence to be justifiable, one would have to envisage a situation where a person, bent on carrying out a criminal assault on another, stops to think of what the civil consequences might be if he or she is unsuccessful in that assault, and comes off worse at the hands of the proposed victim, providing always that his or her victim has used excessive self defence. Such a scenario is, we suggest, a trifle unlikely.

[32]   Particularly where the defendant - had he used excessive self defence - might have been liable for criminal assault himself.

[33]   See above, Part IV for our discussion of the concept of "consistency".

that the outcome of the existing English cases on illegality in tort to be incorrect, we fear that if the law is not reformed in a way that directs the court to consider the rationales for the defence that we have identified in Part IV, inappropriate and unjustifiable decisions may occur.

5.28   At the end of Part III we noted the view of Kostal that by comparing recent case law on illegality in tort in Australia and Canada, one can see a significant divergence of judicial opinion on the proper ambit of the duty of care, the Australian decisions being "openly hostile to an expansive liability in negligence", the Canadian position being "overwhelmingly favourable to expansive liability".[34] This suggests that our concerns about the proper scope of the illegality defence in tort, particularly regarding compensation for personal injury, raise fundamental questions that need discussion.

5.29   This seems to be the view of some commentators. Thus Trindade and Cane write:

> Confusion about the proper role of tort law - is it to compensate plaintiffs? or to give effect to judgments about fault by compensating plaintiffs in appropriate circumstances? or to deter culpable conduct? - comes to a head in this area.[35]

5.30   The debate to which they refer is certainly not one which can be resolved within the scope of this paper, if at all. We take the provisional view that, fortunately, it is not necessary to come to conclusions on these fundamental questions in order to come to some answer to the question of when the court should refuse all assistance to the claimant.

5.31   First, whatever the justification or the force of liability in tort in general as a deterrent, we have already suggested that as a simple practical question, the illegality defence is unlikely to be a deterrent save in exceptional circumstances.

5.32   Secondly, we do not think the defence raises the whole question of the role of fault in tort. We are dealing only with the question of the claimant's own fault, not that of the defendant. We have suggested that the relative fault of the two does not seem to be a relevant issue under current law[36] and we will suggest that it should not be relevant under our proposals.[37] At least in most cases, the relative fault of the claimant can be dealt with under the doctrine of contributory negligence.[38] Thus determining the appropriate scope of the illegality defence does not, we think, require an answer to the general question of the deterrent effect of tort liability.

---

[34]   R Kostal, "Currents in the Counter-Reformation: Illegality and duty of care in Canada and Australia" [1995] Tort LR 100.

[35]   F Trindade and P Cane, *The Law of Torts in Australia* (2nd ed 1993) p 546.

[36]   See above, para 2.42.

[37]   See below, paras 6.36-6.38.

[38]   However, it is true that contributory negligence is not a defence to fraud: see *Standard Chartered Bank v Pakistan National Shipping Corporation and others (No 2)* [2000] 2 Lloyd's Rep 511.

5.33   Nor is it, we think, necessary to take a view on the vexed question of the extent to which the tort system should be based on "fault" rather than "compensation". The questions we have to answer here are to be considered within the framework of the existing law of tort, and the only question posed in this paper is what degree of fault on the part of the claimant should deprive him or her of a remedy despite the fault on the part of the defendant. This is a question of judgment on which views may differ, certainly, and the differences may be influenced by various opinions on how important it is to provide compensation. However it is our provisional view that it is possible to reach a view on this which, within the existing framework of the law, will find general acceptance. We will suggest that the defence should only apply if to allow the claim (in full or in part where the Law Reform (Contributory Negligence) Act 1945 applies) would offend the rationales we have stated, and in particular if it would tend to undermine the rule which made the claimant's conduct illegal, or would render the law "inconsistent".[39]

5.34   In Part II we discussed the possibility of compensation being available under schemes operated by the Criminal Injuries Compensation Authority and the Motor Insurers' Bureau. It may be possible to argue the existence of these provisions provides support for the existence of the illegality doctrine in the personal injury cases. However, it is equally possible to argue that the converse is true. The policy behind denial of relief under the CICA Scheme seems to be encapsulated in the words of Popplewell J in *R v Criminal Injuries Compensation Board, ex p Thomas:*[40]

> The purpose behind the Scheme must necessarily be that those who are involved in criminal activity should not receive money from the public purse for an injury which they have sustained.[41]

Generally, a successful civil claim by a person who has been injured in the course of acting illegally does not result in money being paid out from the "public" purse: the award of damages comes from an individual (or insurance company). We do not think, therefore, that the existence of the 'criminal conviction' bar under this Scheme provides strong support for the use of the doctrine to bar personal injury claims. Moreover, we suggest that the power to bar a claim under the Scheme may actually strengthen the need for reform of the illegality doctrine. As we have noted in this paper, we do not think there is a good case for *generally* barring someone from recovering for personal injury, despite the fact that they have been involved in illegality. Under the current system, it could potentially be that a claimant could not only lose a civil claim, but also a CICA one, based on illegality, leaving a person with potentially serious physical injury totally without recompense, other than State benefits.[42] We are not convinced that this is fair.

---

[39]   See below, Part VI.

[40]   [1995] PIQR P99.

[41]   *Ibid,* at p 101.

[42]   It would be possible for a claims officer to make *some* award under the CICA scheme, even though a tort claim were barred, but such a situation would be rare. The aspects of illegality

(ii) "No reliance" cases

5.35 The other class of case over which we have some doubts are those in which the claimant is allowed to recover on the ground that, in order to make his or her claim, that person does not have to rely on his or her illegal act. We suggested earlier that this rule seems to be subject to a number of exceptions which may mean that it will not in fact be applied when to do so would be "inconsistent" with other parts of the law.[43] But to the extent that the rule may be applied without qualification, we think it is open to exactly the same criticisms that we made of *Tinsley v Milligan*[44] in Consultation Paper No 154: the outcome of the case is left to depend on procedural points which may be fortuitous.[45] We noted in the consultation paper that the arbitrariness of this principle has been the source of considerable judicial and academic criticism.[46]

3. CONCLUSION

5.36 Our provisional view is that reform of the illegality doctrine as it applies to tort is desirable despite the fact that it would have little impact on the outcome of most decided cases. First, there is the question of consistency between regimes. Secondly, there is the unclear approach taken by the courts: judging from the width of the *dicta* in several cases, there is a need to limit the application of the doctrine only to those areas where it can be justified on policy grounds. Thirdly, there is the need to ensure that the reasoning used by the courts correlates more closely to those policies[47] and to ensure that unjustifiable extensions of the defence are not made.

5.37 **We ask whether consultees agree that a general reform of the illegality defence in tort is desirable. If consultees do not agree with us, is there any particular aspect of the law relating to the effect of illegality in tort which they consider is in need of reform?**

---

that can be taken into account in a CICA hearing are wider than would feature in a successful invocation of the illegality defence in a civil action, as the operation of the CICA scheme is discretionary.

[43] See above, paras 2.17-2.18.

[44] [1994] 1 AC 340.

[45] See Consultation Paper No 154, paras 3.21-3.22.

[46] See Consultation Paper No 154, para 3.23 nn 58 and 59.

[47] There have been some instances where the court has suggested the policies that have influenced its consideration of the doctrine, and we suggest that this helpful approach should be encouraged within the courts. See, eg, the comments of Buxton LJ when *refusing* to invoke illegality to bar a claim in the case of *Reeves v Commissioner of Police of the Metropolis* [1999] QB 169, 185:

> To grant relief in our case does not assist or encourage either [the deceased] or others in his situation to continue in their disapproved conduct; and even less is that the effect of the grant of relief to [his] representatives. Nor even are others in [his] position encouraged to act on their representatives' behalf: all that the latter recover is their actual loss, and no element of profit or windfall benefit.

100

PART VI
OPTIONS FOR REFORM

6.1 We now turn to consider the nature of the reform which we will provisionally propose for the illegality doctrine in tort. In the sections that follow we suggest that the rules of illegality that currently operate in tort should be replaced by a structured statutory discretion. We suggest that the court should be required to make its decision in the light of a number of factors, and that it should apply an over-arching test. We then consider the factors which we believe the court should be required to take into account in exercising that discretion. Lastly, we consider whether there should be a starting point for the exercise of that discretion.

1. JUDICIAL REFORM

6.2 We could suggest that reform be carried out by the judiciary developing the common law in a piecemeal fashion: this was a course suggested by some of the participants at the consultation seminar. Is there any realistic likelihood of such reform? All the recent tort cases that have involved illegality have been at Court of Appeal level or lower, so potentially there is scope for reform by the House of Lords.[1] However, we do not think that this is likely to happen. It seems to us that one of the reasons that the recent cases have not gone to the House of Lords is that many have been decided on grounds additional to the illegality point.[2] If a claimant has lost his or her case on a number of grounds, the decision on the illegality point is unlikely to be challenged beyond the Court of Appeal unless there is a chance that an appeal will succeed in respect of all of those grounds. Thus the chances of an appropriate case reaching the House of Lords - and therefore reaching the court most likely to achieve a general reform of the law - are slight.[3] It also seems unlikely, given its decision in *Tinsley v Milligan*,[4] that the House of Lords would be willing to adopt an approach which would give the courts the sort of discretion that we think is needed.

6.3 Moreover, when viewed in conjunction with our provisional proposals for reform of contract and trusts law - which involved us suggesting legislative reform - we think there is a stronger case for legislative reform in tort than for judicial reform. We stated in Part V that we thought that the need to avoid two different systems

---

[1] Given that many of the reported cases are decisions of the Court of Appeal, we believe that an authoritative wholescale restatement or reform of the law would have to come from the House of Lords, rather than through another decision of the Court of Appeal.

[2] See, eg, *Gray and another v Barr (Prudential Assurance Co Ltd, third party)* [1971] 2 QB 554 (indemnity for killing not within terms of insurance policy); *Meah v McCreamer and others (No 2)* [1986] 1 All ER 943 (remoteness); *Clunis v Camden and Islington Health Authority* [1998] QB 978 (duty of care); *Cross v Kirkby, The Times* 5 April 2000 (self-defence); *Sacco v Chief Constable of South Wales Constabulary* (unreported) 15 May 1998 (*volenti non fit injuria*, duty of care).

[3] The Appellate Committee of the House of Lords has recently dismissed a petition by the claimant in *Cross v Kirkby, ibid* for leave to appeal.

[4] [1994] 1 AC 340.

for overlapping claims was an important one. If we are provisionally proposing that contract and trusts be reformed by the introduction of a statutory discretion, it makes sense to us to include tort in that reform, even if we would not necessarily have been minded to provisionally propose legislative reform had we been considering tort on its own.[5]

6.4 **We ask consultees whether they agree with us that reform would be best achieved by legislation rather than judicial reform of the common law. If they do not agree with us, we ask them to explain why not.**

2. REFORM BY LEGISLATION

6.5 We think that reform should come by way of the court being given a statutory discretion to disallow a claim when the claim arises from, or is in any way connected to, an illegal act on the part of the claimant. However, that discretion should only be exercised having taken into account the rationales underlying the illegality doctrine and a number of important factors. We are also provisionally attracted to the idea of a presumption in favour of the validity of the claim, which the defendant should have to rebut.[6]

(1) Why a discretion?

6.6 We made the point in Consultation Paper No 154 that it was difficult to formulate a set of rules that could adequately replace those operating in contract and trusts.[7] The consultation paper criticised the inability of the law relating to contract and trusts to take into account factors such as seriousness.[8] There is such a range of factors that should be taken into account in considering a case that we think the matter can only properly be dealt with by using a discretion: a factor such as "seriousness" cannot be subject to a series of rules. Drawing up a finite list of offences that are or are not sufficiently serious to bar a claim would not work - it would not allow for the varying factual circumstances of a case, and would have the potential for arbitrary operation.

6.7 In response to our provisional proposal in Consultation Paper No 154 that the law of contract and trusts be reformed by the introduction of a structured discretion, the majority of consultees who responded on this point were broadly supportive of our proposals.[9] However, we also note that there were a number of dissenting

---

[5] See above, para 1.4.

[6] Or the court, if raised of its own motion. See above, para 2.2 n 8.

[7] Consultation Paper No 154, paras 7.2 and 8.19.

[8] See, eg, *ibid*, at para 5.4.

[9] In the recent Court of Appeal case of *Al-Kishtaini v Shanshal, The Times* 8 March 2001, it was said that our provisionally proposed discretion set out in the consultation paper would:

> in general be an improvement on the inflexibilities of the present common law rules. (*per* Rix LJ, from transcript)

voices. A fear of unpredictability was one of the main themes expressed against our provisional proposal.[10]

6.8　We think that the concerns that we raised in Consultation Paper No 154 are also important within the tort context[11] and that similar difficulties exist in respect of them. We have already noted that there is a wide variety of factual situations in the tort cases, and we think that it is vital that the court is given a degree of structured discretion in order properly to consider whether in each individual case it would be appropriate to invoke the doctrine.[12]

(2) The nature of the discretion

6.9　When we discussed the draft of this consultation paper at the consultation seminar, a number of people expressed concern at our proposal to give the court a discretion. They thought that it was not appropriate to give the court the sort of discretion that could only be reviewed by appellate courts in limited circumstances, such as on the basis of "*Wednesbury* unreasonableness".[13]

6.10　There are many instances throughout the law of the court having discretionary power. Some discretions give little or no guidance on how they are to be operated, such as that relating to the award of a "just sum" under the Law Reform (Frustrated Contracts) Act 1943.[14] Others give a detailed list of factors to be taken

---

[10]　For two examples of academic comment on this aspect of our provisional proposals, see R A Buckley, "Illegal Transactions: Chaos or Discretion?" (2000) 20 LS 155, 166-168 and N Enonchong, "Illegal Transactions: The Future?" [2000] RLR 82, 88-93.

[11]　It seems that the courts may pay more regard to the seriousness of the illegality in a tort case than when dealing with a contract case. See above, paras 2.56-2.58.

[12]　We note that the impact of illegal conduct on the award of compensation under the CICA Scheme is decided by way of discretion, although the range of factors which can be taken into account is wider than that currently affecting the tort cases. See above, paras 2.69-2.70.

[13]　*Associated Provincial Picture Houses Ltd v Wednesbury Corporation* [1948] 1 KB 223. See H W R Wade and C F Forsyth, *Administrative Law* (8th ed 2000) p 366:

> Unreasonableness has...become a generalised rubric covering not only sheer absurdity or caprice, but merging into illegitimate motives and purposes, a wide category of errors commonly described as 'irrelevant considerations', and mistakes and misunderstandings which can be classed as self-misdirection, or addressing oneself to the wrong question. But the language used in the cases shows that, while the abuse of discretion has this variety of differing legal facets, in practice the courts will often treat them as distinct. When several of them will fit the case, the court is often inclined to invoke them all. The one principle that unites them is that powers must be confined within the true scope and policy of the Act. (Footnotes omitted).

[14]　See the comments of Lawton LJ in *BP Exploration Co (Libya) Ltd v Hunt (No 2)* [1981] 1 WLR 232, 237-238:

> What was difficult was the assessment of the sum which the court considered just, having regard to all the circumstances of the case. Save for what is mentioned in paragraphs (a) and (b) [of the Act], *the subsection gives no help as to how, or upon what principles, the court is to make its assessment or as to what factors it is to take into account.* The responsibility lies with the judge: he has to fix a sum which he, not an appellate court, *considers* just. This word connotes the mental processes going to forming an opinion. What is just is what the trial judge thinks is just. That being so,

into account, such as when the court has to decide whether an exemption clause is "fair and reasonable" under the Unfair Contract Terms Act 1977 (UCTA).[15] When we provisionally propose a discretion, we mean one closer to that exercised under UCTA, rather than an unguided, open discretion.

6.11 We think it is important that a court has some degree of flexibility when deciding the impact of illegality on a claim, but that the flexibility be controlled. This is necessary in order to overcome the concerns we noted earlier with the way the law currently operates in tort: the complicated and confused series of rules makes it difficult to predict outcomes and risks real or apparent arbitrariness. We envisage replacing those rules with a statutory scheme whereby the court has to make a decision based on the application of a number of factors, which we discuss below. What is important is that the court is not given a 'blanket' discretion to decide a case in any way it thinks fit, with no guiding principles or factors. It may be that it was this sort of open-ended discretion that concerned those who spoke against a discretion at the seminar.

6.12 When we provisionally proposed a discretion for contracts and trusts in Consultation Paper No 154 we thought that the court should simply be given a discretion, which it would exercise taking into account a number of factors. Since the publication of that paper, and the receipt of responses, we have developed our thinking, at least in relation to tort. We have noted in this paper that we believe there should be a close connection between the application of the illegality doctrine and the rationales that underlie it. In order to achieve this, we think that the court should be directed to take into account the rationales we have identified in Part IV of this paper, together with the factors we outline below, when deciding how to exercise its discretion. In other words, we think that for illegality there should be an 'over-arching' test, the court being directed to ask itself whether the claim should be allowed or disallowed in the light of the rationales underlying the doctrine and taking into account the guiding factors that we outline below. This would probably mean that the rationales for the existence of the doctrine would have to be included in the statute, as well as the guiding factors. To that extent the test would be similar to that in UCTA, where the court is required to decide whether a term is "fair and reasonable" in the light of guiding considerations set out in the statute.

6.13 Thus, in exercising its discretion, we would expect the court to reflect the policy rationale or rationales appropriate for the case. If, for example, in the light of the guiding factors,[16] the facts were such that to allow the claim would result in inconsistency (in the sense we discussed in Part IV), then the discretion should be exercised so as to bar the claim. If it would not be inconsistent to allow the claim

an appellate court is not entitled to interfere with his decision unless it is so plainly wrong that it cannot be just. The concept of what is just is not an absolute one. Opinions among right thinking people may, and probably will, differ as to what is just in a particular case. No one person enjoys the faculty of infallibility as to what is just. (First emphasis added).

[15] See s 11(2) and Schedule 2. See *Chitty on Contracts* (28th ed 1999) para 14-082.

[16] See below, paras 6.23-6.45.

(and none of the other rationales applied), then illegality should not bar the claim. Although the decision will be one for the trial judge, we think that if proper attention is paid to the guiding factors, and the rationales behind the doctrine, then the risk of unjustifiable decisions being reached is reduced.

6.14 In *George Mitchell (Chesterhall) Ltd v Finney Lock Seeds Ltd*[17] Lord Bridge expressed the view that such a decision under UCTA cannot accurately be described as the exercise of a discretion.[18] Equally, it might in some ways be more accurate not to describe what we have in mind for illegality as the court exercising of a discretion. A better description might be that the court, when faced with a claim involving illegality, should make an 'assessment' of whether, in the light of the factors to be taken into account, the rationales for the doctrine of illegality require that the claim be allowed or disallowed. However, because we have used the phrase in Consultation Paper No 154, we continue in this paper to describe what we have in mind as a "structured discretion".

6.15 It is true that even a structured discretion with an over-arching test and factors to be taken into account will leave a good deal of latitude to the court, but this is both the case under existing law and inevitable. It also means that an appellate court may be reluctant to interfere with the decision at first instance. As Lord Bridge said of UCTA in *George Mitchell (Chesterhall) Ltd v Finney Lock Seeds Ltd*:

> [A] decision under any of the provisions referred to will have this in common with the exercise of a discretion, that, in having regard to the various matters to which the...Act[s]...direct attention, the court must entertain a whole range of considerations, put them in the scales on one side or the other, and decide at the end of the day on which side the balance comes down. There will sometimes be room for a legitimate difference of judicial opinion as to what the answer should be, where it will be impossible to say that one view is demonstrably wrong and the other demonstrably right. It must follow, in my view, that, when asked to review such a decision on appeal, the appellate court should treat the original decision with the utmost respect and refrain from interference with it unless satisfied that it proceeded upon some erroneous principle or was plainly and obviously wrong.[19]

6.16 Although we anticipate that an appellate court reviewing an exercise of the structured discretion which we provisionally propose will take a similar approach, failure on the part of the trial judge to take into account a factor that the statute required him or her to take into account, such as the seriousness of the illegality, for example, would be something that could be considered at appellate level (as would making a disproportionate or an irrational decision). The discretion we provisionally propose is a confined one. Requiring the court to take these factors into account would go some way, we believe, to counter fears that we are

---

[17] [1983] 2 AC 803, 815.

[18] Although this characterisation has been debated by academic commentators: see J Adams and R Brownsword, "The Unfair Contract Terms Act: A Decade of Discretion" (1988) 104 LQR 94, 94-95.

[19] [1983] 2 AC 803, 815-816.

provisionally proposing to give the court a power to do whatever it liked: this is not what we intend.

6.17 There are, of course, significant differences between the assessment of the fairness of contractual terms and the application of the illegality defence in tort. We seek only to provide an example of an existing area of law where the court has to reach a decision based on the application of a number of factors. Viewed against this background, our provisional proposal that the court be given a discretion to be exercised in the light of a number of factors is not a novel one.

6.18 Treating the rationales in this way might have some effect on the operation of the defence of illegality, or at least on the way in which it is seen to operate. We stated earlier that we thought the policies of "dignity", "deterrence" and "no-profit" would in reality be of very rare application to a tort case, particularly to a negligence-based personal injury claim. Thus the "consistency" rationale might turn out to be the crucial one in a considerable proportion of cases. For the illegality defence to apply to a tort claim, the court would generally have to consider that the decision to allow the claim in tort would be "inconsistent" with the provisions making the act illegal or the rules laying down the consequences of the illegality.

6.19 We tend to agree with the suggestions of judges from Canada[20] and New Zealand,[21] and hints in the English cases,[22] that it is not inconsistent to allow a party who in the course of some illegal conduct was injured through the negligence or worse of the defendant to recover for personal injuries. The claimant is not seeking to profit from his or her crime and the award would not undermine any criminal penalty which may be imposed, or have been imposed. We do not think that a court would hold such illegal conduct to be inconsistent with the civil claim, and hence an exercise of discretion to disbar the claim could not be justified. We repeat that we seek the views of consultees on the rationales we have identified in Part IV of this paper. When we discuss having some form of over-arching test,[23] it is our provisional view that the "consistency" requirement should feature significantly in this.

6.20 Subject to the views of consultees, we think that it would also be sensible to consider whether this more developed form of provisionally proposed discretion would also be appropriate for contract and trusts, and we would welcome the views of consultees on this matter.

6.21 **We therefore provisionally propose that the current law relating to illegality in tort should be reformed by giving the court a discretion to bar**

---

[20] Most notably McLachlin J in *Hall v Hebert* [1993] 2 SCR 159, 176. See above, para 3.35.

[21] Interpreting the Accident Compensation Act 1982. See above, paras 3.49-3.51.

[22] See the remarks of Evans LJ quoted above, para 2.23.

[23] See above, para 6.12.

a claim when the claim arises from, or is in any way connected to, an illegal act on the part of the claimant. We ask consultees:

(1) whether they agree that reform should be by way of a structured discretion to allow or disallow the claim in the light of the relevant factors, and

(2) whether they also agree that there should be some form of 'overarching' test, with the court being required to ask itself whether, in the light of the rationales underlying the doctrine and the guiding factors, the claim should be allowed or disallowed.

If consultees disagree with our proposed method of reform we ask them to explain how reform could best be achieved.

6.22 If consultees are in favour of our provisional proposals, we would welcome views as to whether our provisionally proposed discretion for contract and trusts should be developed in a similar way to that for tort.

(3) Factors to be taken into account in exercising the discretion

6.23 What factors should the court be required to take into account in reaching its decision? The formulation of these factors is very important, for the reasons we have discussed above. In Consultation Paper No 154 we suggested that, for the reform of contract and trusts, the criteria should be (a) the seriousness of the illegality; (b) the knowledge and intention of the plaintiff or illegal trust beneficiary; (c) whether refusing to allow the claim or the invalidity of the trust would act as a deterrent; (d) whether refusing the claim would further the purpose of the rule which renders the contract or trust illegal, and (e) whether denying relief would be proportionate to the illegality involved. There was broad agreement with our suggested list, although some consultees doubted the value of deterrence, some noted problems with evaluating "seriousness", and others questioned whether the list of factors should be non-exhaustive, or weighted. We invited consultees to suggest other factors that they thought should be taken into account by the courts.[24] We received a number of suggestions, including (of those which are not specific to contracts or trusts) (a) the knowledge and intention of the *defendant* as well as the claimant; (b) the relative fault or conduct of the parties, and (c) any other sanctions that may or will be imposed.

6.24 The majority of those who responded to Consultation Paper No 154 on the question of discretion were supportive of our proposals, although some consultees criticised our proposed factors as being too vague to assist in predictability. In the light of these responses, we first consider whether these factors are as appropriate for tort as we suggested that they are for contract and trusts. We then ask whether there are any other factors that might be relevant in this context, such as, for example, the closeness of connection between the injury and the illegality, and whether we should incorporate any of the further factors suggested by consultees

---

[24] Consultation Paper No 154, paras 7.43 and 8.63.

in respect of contract and trusts. We particularly seek the views of consultees on our provisionally proposed (or other) factors, given that we view these factors as a vital part of controlling the exercise of the discretion, as the court will be directed to take them into account in deciding whether, in the light of the rationales, the claim should be allowed or disallowed.

(i) The seriousness of the illegality

6.25 We noted in the consultation paper that the underlying policies that we had set out therein bore far greater weight where the illegality was serious.[25] The same can be said in respect of the reconsidered policy rationales set out in Part IV of this paper. The seriousness of the illegality is also taken into account in the current tort cases - indeed, we do not consider the use of the illegality doctrine in tort to have resulted in the same potential for unjust decisions that its operation in contract has sometimes given rise to because the courts seem take a much more pragmatic view of the seriousness of the illegality when deciding whether a tortious claim should be barred.[26] We think it appropriate that the courts should continue to be able to consider the seriousness of the claimant's illegality as part of the proposed discretion in tort. The seriousness of the claimant's illegality is a factor that is relevant to all of the underlying policies outlined in Part IV. We do not believe there is anything else that can be done to assist the court in assessing this important factor. It would be possible to indicate the types of offences most likely to be regarded as serious, but we are doubtful whether this would be particularly helpful.[27]

(ii) The knowledge and intention of the claimant

6.26 We explained in the consultation paper in the context of contract and trusts that we consider that the knowledge and intention of the claimant must play a central role in deciding whether the policy reasons lying behind the illegality doctrine can be relevant in any particular case.[28] We think this aspect is also important for tort: a number of cases depend on, and most of the policy arguments would be affected by, the fact that the claimant either knew what he or she was doing was illegal, or else was 'innocent'.[29]

---

[25] *Ibid,* at para 7.32.

[26] See above, paras 2.56-2.58.

[27] Clearly, offences such as murder, manslaughter or rape are likely to be regarded as serious ones, but the difficulties lie in trying to define the border with less serious offences. Drawing up a finite list of "serious" offences would risk being either be too narrow or too comprehensive. See above, para 6.6.

[28] Consultation Paper No 154, para 7.36.

[29] Eg, the plaintiff's degree of responsibility was clearly crucial in *Clunis v Camden and Islington Health Authority* [1998] QB 978: see the judgment of Beldam LJ *ibid,* at pp 978-989. See above, para 2.15 n 42.

(iii) Whether denying relief would act as a deterrent

6.27 We have already explained that we do not think that deterrence will often be decisive in leading the court to exercise the discretion to disallow the tort claim.[30] Nonetheless we accept that deterrence is one of the policy rationales that lie behind the doctrine of illegality and may be important in certain types of case. Therefore we suggest that this should be a factor included in those that go to structure the discretion, although we envisage that it will seldom be used to justify preventing a tort claim from succeeding.

(iv) Whether denying relief would further the purpose of the rule which renders the claimant's conduct illegal

6.28 We discussed this factor in the Consultation Paper No 154,[31] where we said in the context of contract and trusts that we believed a court should have in mind the purpose of the rule which rendered the contract or trust illegal. We believe that this factor should also apply in the case of illegality affecting tort,[32] and that the court should look to the purpose of the rule that renders the claimant's conduct illegal. We have not formed a final view on whether this should be a factor in its own right, or whether it should form part of a "consistency" factor. We expand on this point, and its relationship with the concept of consistency, below.

(v) Whether denying relief would be proportionate to the illegality involved

6.29 In the consultation paper we thought that proportionality as between the effect of denying the claimant relief and the illegality should be a factor in exercising the discretion for both contract and trusts cases,[33] and this suggestion received support from a number of consultees. These comments were made on the basis that we accepted that punishment was a valid policy rationale underlying the doctrine of illegality. Although we now no longer consider punishment to be a good justification for the illegality doctrine, we still believe that proportionality should be a relevant factor for the court to take into account, for example, to ensure that being deprived of rights is not disproportionate to the seriousness of the illegality.[34] Thus we agree with the suggestion made by some commentators that the relevance of proportionality should lie in the court being able to look at the seriousness of the claimant's wrongdoing in deciding whether he or she should be compensated for the damage sustained.[35] It may be said to be of even more importance if it is accepted that punishment is not a valid policy: where punishment is not acceptable for the existence of a doctrine the court should be

---

[30] See above, paras 4.31-4.33.

[31] Consultation Paper No 154, paras 7.39-7.40.

[32] See above, paras 4.56-4.59.

[33] See Consultation Paper No 154, paras 7.41-7.42 and 8.60-8.62.

[34] See above, paras 1.5-1.8 and 2.59-2.61.

[35] See *Clerk and Lindsell on Torts* (18th ed 2000) para 3-19.

particularly alive to prevent that doctrine having a disproportionate effect that would render it punitive.[36]

6.30 **We ask whether consultees agree with our provisional view that:**

    (1)   the seriousness of the illegality,

    (2)   the knowledge and intention of the claimant,

    (3)   whether denying relief would act as a deterrent,

    (4)   whether denying relief would further the purpose of the rule which renders the claimant's conduct illegal, and

    (5)   whether denying relief would be proportionate to the illegality involved

should be factors to be taken into account in exercising the discretion. We also ask consultees whether there is anything that can be done to make any of them more certain.

(4) Other factors?

(i) Closeness of connection

6.31 In Part II[37] we pointed out that one of the devices used by the courts to limit the application of the illegality defence in tort is to apply it only where the illegal act was directly linked to the claim. The closeness or otherwise of the connection is, we think, relevant to the rationales we have described in Part IV. We therefore provisionally propose that, at least for the statutory discretion to apply in tort cases, the degree of connection between the illegal act and the facts giving rise to the claim should be a relevant factor.

6.32 This would not necessarily mean that the list of factors for tort cases has to be different to that for contract and trusts. There are cases in which this is a relevant factor in contract or trusts cases - for example, when a contract is arguably for an illegal purpose, it may be relevant how closely the contract and the illegal purpose are linked.[38] Thus this could be added as a factor for contract and trust cases also.

6.33 **Do consultees agree with our provisional view that the court should be required to consider the degree of connection between the illegal act and**

---

[36]   It may be that proportionality becomes an increasingly important element in the review by the courts of discretionary decisions. See, eg, the discussion on this point in P Craig, *Administrative Law* (4th ed 1999) pp 585-603. As to the relationship between proportionality, *Wednesbury* unreasonableness and human rights law, see, eg, R Clayton and H Tomlinson, *The Law of Human Rights* (2000) vol 1, paras 5.126-5.131. Also, see the comments in *White v White and another* [2001] 1 WLR 481 noted above at para 2.71 n 178.

[37]   See above, paras 2.53-2.55.

[38]   Cf *Pearce v Brooks* (1866) LR 1 Ex 213 and *Lloyd v Johnson* (1798) 1 B & P 340, and see the cases on "tainting" discussed in *Chitty on Contracts* (28th ed 1999) para 17-159.

the facts giving rise to the claim? Do they also agree with us that this factor should be used in contract and trusts cases?

(ii) Knowledge of the defendant

6.34   Several consultees suggested that the court should have the power to look at the knowledge and intention of the defendant as well as the claimant. We are of the provisional view that this should not be a factor. The defendant's state of mind is not relevant if one accepts the traditional view that the doctrine is not designed for the benefit of the defendant, but is a power to stop a claimant from succeeding, nor does it seem to fit easily with the rationales identified in Part IV. In any event, we are not sure that the defendant's state of mind would prove to be a decisive factor in most tort claims, where negligence is being alleged.

6.35   **Our provisional view therefore is that the knowledge and intention of the defendant should not be a factor in the exercise of the discretion in tort cases. We ask consultees whether they agree with us, and if not, on what basis they feel the court should be given the power to take into account the knowledge and intention of the defendant.**

(iii) Proportionality as between claimant and defendant

6.36   Under the "public conscience" test proportionality between the claimant's wrongdoing and the defendant's conduct seems to have been a feature of the tort cases.[39] We have suggested that this aspect of the "public conscience" test does not seem to have survived the decision of the House of Lords in *Tinsley v Milligan*.[40] Nor is it consistent with the purpose of the illegality defence being not for the benefit of the defendant, but to prevent the claimant from recovering because of his or her illegal conduct. The focus of the court's attention should therefore be on the claimant's conduct, not the defendant's.[41] Equally, we think that the question of proportionality as between claimant and defendant does not fit comfortably with the various possible rationales for the illegality defence that we have identified, and therefore we do not propose that it should be listed as a relevant factor.

6.37   However, we are very conscious that, if the courts are in fact swayed by this factor under the present law, there is a likelihood that it will also be taken into account under the proposed statutory discretion, which will of necessity be sufficiently flexible to allow the court to take into account any factor it thinks relevant, unless explicitly excluded. If it would be the case that this factor would sway the courts, it seems better either to list it explicitly, or explicitly to exclude it, than to have it operate without being listed. We would welcome consultees' advice on this question.

---

[39]   See above, para 2.34 n 82.

[40]   [1994] 1 AC 340. See above, para 2.42.

[41]   See *Clerk and Lindsell on Torts* (18th ed 2000) para 3-19.

6.38 **We ask consultees whether they think proportionality as between claimant and defendant should be listed as a factor to be taken into account by the court when exercising its discretion, or whether it should be explicitly excluded.**

(iv) Consistency

6.39 To a limited extent, consistency of the law is already a relevant factor. It is almost inevitable that the court will need to take into account consistency as between the regimes dealing with illegality in the various branches of the law. Thus we stated in the consultation paper that:

> Where...the success of a tortious claim depends on, or is concerned with, a transaction, and that transaction is an "illegal transaction" to which our provisional proposals would apply, we anticipate that the courts would take into account the effect of our provisional proposals on the transaction so as to ensure that the effect of illegality on the tortious claim does not produce an inconsistent result.[42]

We think that the court should at least be directed to take into account "consistency" in this limited sense, in that it should ask itself whether, in a tort case, it is really being asked to enforce an illegal contract, for example. We have already stated that we consider the need to ensure that a claimant cannot avoid the consequences of a contract being held illegal by suing in tort to be an important point justifying the continued existence of the illegality doctrine in tort.

6.40 The question remains, however, whether "consistency" in a wider sense, as between different parts of the legal system, should form part of the test.[43] Earlier, we asked whether consultees agreed with our provisional view that the court should be directed to apply the broad test of asking itself whether the claim should be allowed or disallowed in the light of the rationales for the doctrine of illegality, and we thought that "consistency" is an important rationale.[44] If that view is accepted, then consistency will form part of the overall test. The present question is whether, even if that view is *not* accepted, consistency should be added to the list of factors.

6.41 It may be possible to argue - indeed, in Part IV we have suggested already - that some of the factors listed above reflect aspects of the consistency argument. Looking to see whether a denial of relief would further the purpose of the rule which renders the claimant's conduct illegal, for example, seems relevant to this concept, and we have suggested this as a factor earlier in this Part. If to allow the civil claim would frustrate or stultify the rule of law offended against, then there is a risk of inconsistency within the law. In the context of tort cases, we envisage that there are a number of cases in which to allow a claim would not further the

---

[42] Consultation Paper No 154, para 1.3.

[43] See our discussion on the Canadian case of *Hall v Hebert* [1993] 2 SCR 159 and the concept of "consistency", above, at paras 3.28-3.47 and 4.56-4.74.

[44] See above, paras 6.12-6.18.

purpose of the rule which made the conduct illegal. The law of manslaughter, for example, would arguably not be furthered were the civil law to allow someone who had been convicted of this offence and been sentenced to detention in hospital to recover damages for the fact of that conviction and detention.[45] The same would be true if a claimant could recover an indemnity for a fine imposed on him or her for his or her criminal behaviour. But it is not every form of illegality which would be inconsistent with recovery arising out of the same facts. Thus we do not think the law of speeding would be frustrated or stultified in any significant way by allowing a negligently injured driver who had been speeding to sue another motorist.[46] If our analysis of the underlying policies discussed in Part IV is accepted as correct, and the policy of consistency does have the explanatory power that we suggest, then it seems appropriate at least to list it as a factor.

6.42 As we noted earlier in this section, it is through requiring the court to take into account a number of guiding factors that we seek to avoid the possible problems related to an open-ended discretion. We ask consultees to consider whether there are any other factors that they think the court should be required to take into account.

6.43 **It is our provisional view that our proposed discretion should be structured around the same factors as for contract and trusts but with the addition at least of the factor of closeness of connection between the claim and the illegal act. However, we also ask consultees whether they think that the factor of "consistency" should be added to the list.**

6.44 **We ask consultees whether they agree with our proposed factors, and to the extent that they do not agree with them we ask them to state what factors they would regard as being appropriate.**

6.45 **We would also welcome views as to whether these factors should be weighted, and if so, how.**

3. AN ALTERNATIVE APPROACH – A REDUCTION IN DAMAGES

6.46 One alternative approach which could be considered is to reform the illegality doctrine in tort so that, instead of providing a complete bar to a claim (or head of damage), the court should be given the power to reduce the damages claimed, to reflect the impact of the illegal conduct on the claim. This might appear to be a similar approach to that taken when dealing with the question of contributory negligence under the Law Reform (Contributory Negligence) Act 1945.[47] Of course, the circumstances of the case may be such that the illegal conduct of the claimant could amount to contributory negligence in any event. The possibility of some form of apportionment was raised at the consultation seminar, but did not

---

[45] See *Clunis v Camden and Islington Health Authority* [1998] QB 978.

[46] Such a situation can probably be adequately dealt with by a reduction of damages on the basis of contributory negligence.

[47] See also the CICA Scheme, under which it is possible to reduce an award as well as to bar it completely. Is this an approach that should be adopted in tort law?

attract detailed comment.[48] We do not think that it properly reflects the rationales behind the illegality doctrine. The doctrine is one that should be used only for extreme cases; to allow the court to treat it in much the same way as contributory negligence would, we feel, risk it developing into a doctrine of more frequent usage. However, we would welcome consultees' views on whether reform in this way would be justifiable or desirable.

6.47 **Our provisional view is that the court should not be given the power to reduce damages in a way similar to that for contributory negligence. We ask whether consultees agree with us, or whether they think there is justification for giving the court power to reduce the claimant's damages on the basis of illegality.**

4. WHAT SHOULD BE THE STARTING POINT OF THE PROVISIONALLY PROPOSED DISCRETION?

6.48 We need to consider what, if any, starting point should be created for the exercise of the discretion. Should a claim be presumed to be valid unless the court declares otherwise, or should it be presumed invalid unless declared otherwise? In Consultation Paper No 154 we considered this question from the point of view of contract and trusts,[49] and asked consultees which of a number of options they preferred as a starting point, or whether it was preferable to have no starting point at all.[50] The responses of consultees were varied on these questions: the majority of those who responded to them were in favour of some form of starting point, with the largest single majority being in favour of the option of the claim being allowed unless the court decided that because of the involvement of illegality it should not be allowed.

6.49 In the light of this response and, given that we regard the illegality doctrine in tort as potentially a harsh one and that we think that it is difficult to justify its application to cases where damages for personal injuries are sought, we provisionally think that it would be preferable to have a starting point for the exercise of the discretion, and that that starting point should be a presumption that the claim will be allowed unless the court declares that because of the involvement of illegality it should not be allowed.[51] The current law appears to be that it is for the defendant to make good the defence of illegality.[52] We would welcome consultees' views on this question.

---

[48] It has also been raised in academic writing. See M Fordham, "The Role of *Ex Turpi Causa* in Tort Law" [1998] SJLS 238, 258-259.

[49] See Consultation Paper No 154, paras 7.44-7.57 and 8.83-8.85.

[50] See *ibid*, at paras 7.57 and 8.85.

[51] However, several participants at the seminar expressed the view that any starting point should be that the claim would not be valid unless the claimant could persuade the court that the illegality should not have an effect on the claim.

[52] See, eg, Buxton LJ in *Reeves v Commissioner of Police of the Metropolis* [1999] QB 169, 186:

6.50   **We ask consultees to consider (a) whether there should be a starting point to the exercise of the provisionally proposed discretion, and if so, (b) whether that starting point should be:**

(1)   **that illegality will act as a successful defence to a claim unless the court declares otherwise; or**

(2)   **that the claimant's claim will be allowed unless the court decides that because of the involvement of illegality it should not be allowed.**

If neither option appeals to consultees, we ask them to state whether there should be another form of starting point.

5. THE RELATIONSHIP OF OUR PROPOSALS FOR TORT WITH THOSE RELATING TO CONTRACT AND TRUSTS

6.51   As has been seen in this Part, our provisional proposals for tort reform are similar to those advanced in the consultation paper relating to contract and trusts (as to which we are still considering our final policy), although our tort proposals are in a more developed form than those for contract and trusts. Our proposals are aimed at correcting ills which are not identical - for contract and trusts, the replacement of a set of technical and complex rules that risk working injustice and are uncertain,[53] and for tort, the replacement of a unclear method of approach - but in each area consist of the introduction of a discretionary power, structured around a number of factors that go to reflect the policies that underlie the existence of the doctrine of illegality. Having developed our thinking on the nature of the discretion in this paper, we have asked consultees whether our provisional proposals for contract and trusts would benefit from a similar approach.

6.52   The obvious point that would ultimately need to be considered is whether we can have a single set of criteria for exercising the discretion that would be applicable in all the areas we seek to reform, or whether there will need to be separate statutory provisions for different areas. It would be attractive, for reasons of consistency and clarity, to have just one set of criteria. We are not yet decided on whether this would be possible, though as yet we do not see any insuperable objection.

6.53   This is even the case if the criterion of "consistency" were to be added to the list of factors, or as one element - possibly the most important one - in an over-arching test. We have discussed in this paper the concept of consistency as a policy rationale for tort. Although we are not sure as to how useful an explanatory concept it would be in the context of contract and trusts (where the policy of "no

---

[The judge's approach] appears to reverse the burden of proof on this issue. That is more than a technical point, because the need to make good the extreme claims of affront or outrage is a cardinal necessity of this defence.

We think that the court should also be able to raise the point of its own motion, and decide whether it is satisfied that the illegality point has been made out.

[53]   See Consultation Paper No 154, Part V.

benefit" is far more likely to provide a policy justification[54]), we are not sure that it is in any way inappropriate for contract and trust cases. As we suggested in Part IV of this paper, denying a criminal the benefit of his crime may possibly be seen as an element of consistency,[55] and consistency seems closely linked to the factor already included in the list, whether to deny relief will further the purpose of the rule which renders the contract illegal.[56]

6.54 **We would be interested in the views of consultees on either the desirability or the practicality of having a single set of criteria for contract, tort and trusts cases.**

6. THE EFFECT OF OUR PROVISIONAL PROPOSALS

6.55 We now briefly turn to consider what effect our provisional proposals might have in practice. We have chosen not to list a number of cases individually and consider them in turn under the regime of our provisionally proposed discretion, as we have already made the point that a large number of reported cases were decided on more than one ground, not just that of illegality, and so the final outcomes of those cases if repeated on the facts would often be the same regardless of any change in the law on illegality.[57]

6.56 The illegality defence might be applied less frequently to cases in which the claimant, during the course of some illegal activity, suffered injury through the negligence or other wrongdoing of the defendant. As we have said, this would not affect the outcome were the facts of any case so far decided to recur, since in each one the claim would fail on other grounds such as absence of duty or acceptance of risk. Our provisional view is that applying the illegality defence in this class of case is hard to justify and risks the extension of its application to cases which are factually similar but in which there is no alternative ground on which to justify the decision.

6.57 As most of the other applications of the illegality defence can be explained by reference to the underlying rationales as we considered them to be in Part IV, we would expect most cases to be decided the same way by a court operating a structured discretion. For example, cases where the claimant was seeking to recover damages in respect of his or her imprisonment or detention would continue to be barred.[58]

---

[54] See *ibid*, at paras 6.7-6.8.

[55] See above, para 4.70.

[56] See above, paras 4.56-4.59.

[57] See above, para 2.73.

[58] Thus the claims in cases such as *Clunis v Camden and Islington Health Authority* [1998] QB 978 and *Worrall v British Railways Board* (unreported) 29 April 1999 would still probably be barred. We think that *Meah v McCreamer* [1985] 1 All ER 367 would be decided differently under the discretion, so as to prevent the claim. However, this conclusion may not be surprising, given that the correctness of this decision was doubted by Beldam LJ giving the judgment of the Court of Appeal in *Clunis v Camden and Islington Health Authority* (*ibid*, at p 990) and again by that same judge in *Worrall v British Railways Board*.

6.58   We would also expect cases where the claimant was seeking an indemnity for sums he or she had to pay out as a result of the criminal conduct to be barred, as in the case of *Meah v McCreamer and others (No 2)*.[59] However, the facts of this case do raise a point for consideration. The plaintiff was seeking an indemnity in respect of compensation he had to pay to his victims, rather than damages in respect of his own imprisonment. There was a 'pot' of money available to pay compensation in the form of the damages which the plaintiff had received in *Meah v McCreamer*.[60] Thus to prevent the plaintiff recovering an indemnity from the defendant for those compensation payments would not in fact affect the victims of his crime. But what would the situation be if the plaintiff had been *without* money to satisfy the compensation claims? The victims themselves might face problems of remoteness in suing the tortfeasor directly. Would a court faced with these facts, and applying the proposed statutory discretion, decide to allow the claim? Would it further the purpose of the law to disallow the claim, or, alternatively, would there be inconsistency in the law were it to allow the criminal to claim the money solely in order to provide a fund to pay his victims? Would it be better to prevent such a claimant from recovering, which would mean that the innocent victims of his or her crime would go uncompensated and have to look to the CICA, or to allow the claimant to recover from the tortfeasor in order to provide a fund from which compensation could be paid (in which case the real cost would probably fall on the defendant's insurers)?[61] We are not sure of the answers to these questions, and would welcome the views of consultees.

6.59   **We therefore ask consultees whether a claim that would otherwise be defeated by the illegality defence should still fail where this will have the result of the claimant being unable to satisfy compensation payments which he or she has been ordered to pay to the victims of his or her crime.**

---

[59]   [1986] 1 All ER 943.

[60]   [1985] 1 All ER 367.

[61]   There may be parallels between this situation and the case of *Hardy v Motor Insurers' Bureau* [1964] 2 QB 745. See above, para 2.7 n 21.

PART VII
SUMMARY OF PROVISIONAL PROPOSALS AND CONSULTATION ISSUES

7.1 Subject to the views of our consultees, our general provisional proposal is that the current rules that operate in relation to the effect of illegality in tort cases should be replaced by a structured discretion. We set out below a summary of our questions and provisional proposals on which we invite the views of consultees.

(4) Policy Rationales Underlying the Doctrine of Illegality

7.2 Our provisional view is that punishment does not provide a sufficient rationale for the existence of the doctrine of illegality, and that therefore the court should only allow the illegality defence where it can be justified on policy rationales other than punishment. We ask consultees whether they agree with our rejection of punishment as a rationale for the doctrine of illegality. (Paragraph 4.24).

7.3 It is our provisional view that preserving the dignity of the courts may provide a justification for applying the doctrine of illegality in tort cases but only in unusual or extreme circumstances. We ask whether consultees agree with us. (Paragraph 4.27).

7.4 It is our provisional view that deterrence will sometimes, but only rarely, provide a justification for applying the doctrine of illegality in tort cases. We ask whether consultees agree with us. (Paragraph 4.35).

7.5 Our provisional view is that in most tort cases the rationale of preventing a claimant profiting from his or her own wrongdoing will not justify the application of the illegality doctrine, and in particular it will not provide a justification for applying the doctrine in cases where the claim is one for compensation arising out of personal injury. We ask whether consultees agree with our provisional views, and if they do not, we ask them to explain why. (Paragraph 4.47).

7.6 It is our provisional view is that a rationale based on "not condoning the illegal activity or appearing to condone or encourage others" does not provide a satisfactory justification for the illegality doctrine in tort. We ask whether consultees agree with our provisional view, and if they do not, we ask them to explain why. (Paragraph 4.54).

7.7 We ask consultees whether they agree with our provisional view that the concept of "furthering the purpose of the rule" is an important one in providing a justification for the application of the illegality doctrine in tort cases. (Paragraph 4.59).

7.8 Our provisional view is that the concept of "taking responsibility for one's own actions" does not provide a satisfactory rationale for the existence of the illegality doctrine. However, we would welcome the views of consultees on this proposed rationale. (Paragraph 4.80).

7.9 It is our provisional view that

    (1)   to justify the tort cases it is necessary to develop some further rationale beyond "dignity", "deterrence", "no profit", "no condonation" and "responsibility"; and

    (2)   the best new rationale is that expressed by McLachlin J in *Hall v Hebert*, the need to maintain consistency in the law.

We ask consultees whether they agree with this view, and if not, what they regard as valid justifications for the existence of the doctrine in tort. (Paragraph 4.81).

7.10 We invite consultees' views on the questions:

    (1)   can the denial of a claim for personal injury caused to the claimant by the defendant's negligence or other wrong while the claimant was engaged in some illegal activity be justified by any of the rationales we have identified?

    (2)   If not, are there further rationales by which these cases may be justified? (Paragraph 4.98).

7.11 We would welcome views on whether the same rationales that we have identified for use of the illegality defence in tort cases apply to contract and trust cases - in particular, whether consultees consider that the "consistency" rationale is a useful one to explain the policy which should underlie the illegality defence in contract and trusts. (Paragraph 4.107).

(5) The Case For Reform

7.12 We ask consultees whether they agree with our provisional proposal that a defence of illegality in tort in some form should be retained. (Paragraph 5.7).

7.13 We ask consultees whether they agree with us that there would be a real risk of confusion and inconsistency if the law in relation to contract and trusts were to be reformed by legislation but tort law left unreformed. Do consultees agree with us that this reason is sufficient to put the reform of illegality as it affects tort law on a statutory footing? (Paragraph 5.13).

7.14 We ask whether consultees agree that a general reform of the illegality defence in tort is desirable. If consultees do not agree with us, is there any particular aspect of the law relating to the effect of illegality in tort which they consider is in need of reform? (Paragraph 5.37).

(6) Options For Reform

7.15 We ask consultees whether they agree with us that reform would be best achieved by legislation rather than judicial reform of the common law. If they do not agree with us, we ask them to explain why. (Paragraph 6.4).

7.16 We provisionally propose that the current law relating to illegality in tort should be reformed by giving the court a discretion to bar a claim when the claim arises from, or is in any way connected to, an illegal act on the part of the claimant. We ask consultees:

(1)   whether they agree that reform should be by way of a structured discretion to allow or disallow the claim in the light of the relevant factors, and

(2)   whether they also agree that there should be some form of 'over-arching' test, with the court being required to ask itself whether, in the light of the rationales underlying the doctrine and the guiding factors, the claim should be allowed or disallowed.

If consultees disagree with our proposed method of reform we ask them to explain how reform could best be achieved. (Paragraph 6.21).

7.17   If consultees are in favour of our provisional proposals, we would welcome views as to whether our provisionally proposed discretion for contract and trusts should be developed in a similar way to that for tort. (Paragraph 6.22).

7.18   We ask whether consultees agree with our provisional view that:

(1)   the seriousness of the illegality,

(2)   the knowledge and intention of the claimant,

(3)   whether denying relief would act as a deterrent,

(4)   whether denying relief would further the purpose of the rule which renders the claimant's conduct illegal, and

(5)   whether denying relief would be proportionate to the illegality involved

should be factors to be taken into account in exercising the discretion. We also ask consultees whether there is anything that can be done to make any of them more certain. (Paragraph 6.30).

7.19   Do consultees agree with our provisional view that the court should be required to consider the degree of connection between the illegal act and the facts giving rise to the claim? Do they also agree with us that this factor should be used in contract and trusts cases? (Paragraph 6.34).

7.20   Our provisional view is that the knowledge and intention of the defendant should not be a factor in the exercise of the discretion in tort cases. We ask consultees whether they agree with us, and if not, on what basis they feel the court should be given the power to take into account the knowledge and intention of the defendant. (Paragraph 6.36).

7.21   We ask consultees whether they think proportionality as between claimant and defendant should be listed as a factor to be taken into account by the court when exercising its discretion, or whether it should be explicitly excluded. (Paragraph 6.38).

7.22 It is our provisional view that our proposed discretion should be structured around the same factors as for contract and trusts but with the addition at least of the factor of closeness of connection between the claim and the illegal act. However, we also ask consultees whether they think that the factor of "consistency" should be added to the list. (Paragraph 6.43).

7.23 We ask consultees whether they agree with our proposed factors, and to the extent that they do not agree with them we ask them to state what factors they would regard as being appropriate. (Paragraph 6.44).

7.24 We would also welcome views as to whether these factors should be weighted, and if so, how. (Paragraph 6.45).

7.25 Our provisional view is that the court should not be given the power to reduce damages in a way similar to that for contributory negligence. We ask whether consultees agree with us, or whether they think there is justification for giving the court power to reduce the claimant's damages on the basis of illegality. (Paragraph 6.47).

7.26 We ask consultees to consider (a) whether there should be a starting point to the exercise of the provisionally proposed discretion, and if so, (b) whether that starting point should be:

(1) that illegality will act as a successful defence to a claim unless the court declares otherwise; or

(2) that the claimant's claim will be allowed unless the court decides that because of the involvement of illegality it should not be allowed.

If neither option appeals to consultees, we ask them to state whether there should be another form of starting point. (Paragraph 6.50).

7.27 We would be interested in the views of consultees on either the desirability or the practicality of having a single set of criteria for contract, tort and trusts cases. (Paragraph 6.54).

7.28 We ask consultees whether a claim that would otherwise be defeated by the illegality defence should still fail where this will have the result of the claimant being unable to satisfy compensation payments which he or she has been ordered to pay to the victims of his or her crime. (Paragraph 6.59).

APPENDIX A
SUMMARY OF PROVISIONAL RECOMMENDATIONS AND CONSULTATION ISSUES FROM CONSULTATION PAPER NO 154

A.1   The section that follows reproduces Part VII of Consultation Paper No 154; paragraph references below relate to paragraphs within that paper and footnotes are in the original paper.

(1) Introduction

A.2   Do consultees agree with our provisional view (a) that the law on the effect of illegality in relation to contracts and trusts is in need of reform; and (b) that legislative reform is to be preferred to leaving "reform" to the judiciary through development of the common law? If consultees do not agree, is there any limited area of the law on the effect of illegality which they consider is in need of legislative reform? (paragraph 5.13).

A.3   Do consultees agree with our strong provisional view that it would not be appropriate to adopt the radical approach of dispensing with all special illegality rules and that a distinction should continue to be drawn between illegal transactions and valid transactions? If consultees do not agree, please would they give their reasons. (paragraph 6.12).

(2) Illegal Contracts

The proposed discretion

A.4   Do consultees agree with our provisional view that a court should have a discretion to decide whether or not illegality should act as a defence to a claim for contractual enforcement where the formation, purpose or performance of the contract involves the commission of a legal wrong (other than the mere breach of the contract in question)? If consultees do not agree, we would ask them to explain why not. (paragraph 7.10).

A.5   Do consultees agree with our provisional recommendation that the equitable "clean hands" maxim should have no role to play in cases within the sphere of operation of our provisionally proposed discretion? If consultees do not agree, we would ask them to explain why not. (paragraph 7.12).

A.6   Do consultees agree with our provisional view that a court should not be given a discretion to enforce contracts which do not involve a legal wrong but which the court declares to be otherwise contrary to public policy? That is, the question of the enforcement of such contracts should continue to be governed by the common law. In addition, do consultees agree with our provisional view that a legislative provision should make it clear that the courts are to judge whether a contract is contrary to public policy in the light of policy matters of the present

122

day and that contracts which were previously considered to be contrary to public policy may no longer be so and *vice versa*? If consultees do not agree, please would they explain why not. (paragraph 7.16).

A.7　Do consultees agree with our provisional view that a court should have a discretion to decide whether or not illegality should be recognised as a defence to a claim for the reversal of unjust enrichment in relation to benefits conferred under a contract which is unenforceable for illegality? If consultees do not agree, please would they explain why not. (paragraph 7.22).

A.8　Do consultees agree with our provisional view that (a) a court should have a discretion to decide whether illegality should act as a defence to the recognition of contractually transferred or created property rights where the formation, purpose or performance of the contract involves the commission of a legal wrong (other than the mere breach of the contract in question) or is otherwise contrary to public policy; but (b) that illegality should not invalidate a disposition of property to a third party purchaser for value without notice of the illegality? (paragraph 7.26).

Structuring the discretion

A.9　Do consultees agree with our provisional view that the proposed discretion should be structured so that the court should be required to take into account specific factors in reaching its decision; and that those factors should be: (1) the seriousness of the illegality involved; (2) the knowledge and intention of the plaintiff; (3) whether denying relief will act as a deterrent; (4) whether denying relief will further the purpose of the rule which renders the contract illegal; and (5) whether denying relief is proportionate to the illegality involved? We also ask consultees whether there are any other factors which they consider the courts should take into account in exercising the discretion. If consultees do not agree with our provisional view, we would ask them to explain why not. (paragraph 7.43).

The starting point of the discretion

A.10　Do consultees consider that the starting point of the provisionally proposed discretion should be:
(a) that illegality will act as a defence unless the court declares otherwise;
(b) that the plaintiff's claim will be allowed unless the court decides that because of the involvement of illegality it would not be in the public interest to allow the claim;
(c) one which varies according to whether the claim is for contractual enforcement; restitution pursuant to a contract which has failed for illegality; or the recognition of contractually transferred or created property rights; or
(d) that a claim by a party who has neither carried out nor intends to carry out the illegality will be allowed, unless the court declares otherwise; but a claim by a party who has carried out or intends to carry out the illegality will be refused, unless the court declares otherwise?
Alternatively we ask consultees whether they consider that it would be preferable that no starting point should be expressed. (paragraph 7.57)

Illegality as a restitutionary cause of action: the doctrine of locus poenitentiae

A.11   Do consultees agree with our provisional proposal that:

(a) a court should have a discretion to allow a party to withdraw from an illegal contract, and to have restitution of benefits conferred under it, where allowing the party to withdraw would reduce the likelihood of an illegal act being completed or an illegal purpose being accomplished: but that

(b) to succeed in a withdrawal claim the plaintiff must first satisfy the court that the contract could not be enforced against him or her? (paragraph 7.69).

A.12   Do consultees agree with our provisional proposal that in deciding whether or not to allow a party to withdraw and have restitution a court should consider (i) whether the plaintiff genuinely repents of the illegality (albeit that this should not be a necessary condition for the exercise of the discretion); and (ii) the seriousness of the illegality? (paragraph 7.69).

If consultees disagree with these provisional proposals, we ask them whether they regard withdrawal and restitution on the basis of a "*locus poenitentiae*" as a needless complication that could happily be done away with.

The scope of the provisionally proposed discretion

A.13   Do consultees agree with our provisional recommendation that our proposed statutory discretion in relation to:

(a) contractual enforcement should apply to all contracts which in their formation, purpose or performance involve a legal wrong (other than a mere breach of the contract in question);

(b) the reversal of unjust enrichment should apply to all contracts which are unenforceable for illegality; and

(c) the recognition of contractually transferred or created property rights should apply to all contracts which in their formation, purpose or performance involve a legal wrong (other than a mere breach of the contract in question) or conduct which is otherwise contrary to public policy?[1]

If consultees do not agree, please would they explain what they consider the scope of our proposed discretion should be. (paragraph 7.72).

A discretion to go beyond treating illegality as a defence to standard rights and remedies

A.14   Do consultees agree with our provisional view that (with the exception of the *locus poenitentiae* doctrine) illegality should continue to act only as a defence to claims for standard rights and remedies and that, in particular, the courts should not be specially empowered to apportion losses under illegal contracts? If consultees do not agree, do they consider that a court should have an open-ended discretion to

---

[1]   Although note that we have excluded from the scope of this project contracts which are rendered ineffective by statute but which do not involve any conduct which is expressly or impliedly prohibited (para 1.10 above), and contracts which are in restraint of trade (para 1.11 above).

grant any relief that it considers just in relation to illegal contracts? (paragraph 7.87).

A discretion to make an award on terms that the plaintiff makes a payment of transfers property to a person who is not party to the illegal contract

A.15   Do consultees consider that in contractual disputes involving illegality the courts should be given a discretionary power to allow the plaintiff's claim only on the condition that the plaintiff makes a payment or transfers property to a person (such as the State) who is not a party to the illegal contract? If so, we ask consultees on what basis (that is, punishment or disgorgement of gain or both) they consider such an award should be made. (paragraph 7.93).

The interaction of our provisionally proposed discretion and statutory provisions which deal with the effects of illegality

A.16   Do consultees agree with our provisional view that where a statute expressly lays down what should be the consequences for a contract, of the contract involving a breach of the statute's provisions, our proposed discretion should not apply? If consultees do not agree, do they consider that a court should be able to use our proposed discretion in order to override the provisions of the statute? (paragraph 7.102).

Severance

A.17   Do consultees agree with our provisional view that where (at common law) part of a contract is severed so that the remainder no longer falls within our broad definition of illegality, our proposed discretion should not apply? If consultees do not agree, please would they give their reasons. (paragraph 7.103).

Tainting

A.18   Do consultees agree with our provisional view that the tainting principle is a sensible one and should be retained? If not, do consultees consider that the tainting principle should be abandoned? (paragraph 7.104).

Changes in the law

A.19   Do consultees agree that where a change in the law means that (a) previously lawful conduct becomes unlawful, then the enforcement of any contract involving such conduct should be governed by the rules relating to frustration, rather than our proposed discretion; or (b) previously unlawful conduct becomes lawful (and is not otherwise contrary to public policy), any contract involving such conduct should be enforceable? If consultees do not agree, do they consider that in either case our proposed discretion should apply? (paragraph 7.106).

General question on discretionary approach

A.20   Having set out the details of our provisional proposals, we would ask those consultees who object to any discretionary approach to set out and explain what

125

reforms, if any, they would prefer to make to the rules on illegality in relation to contracts. (paragraph 7.117).

(3) Illegal Trusts

Abandonment of reliance principle

A.21 Do consultees agree with our provisional proposal that the reliance principle should be abandoned as a test of enforceability of a trust? If consultees do not agree, do they consider that the reliance principle is operating satisfactorily, or should be in any way reformed? (paragraph 8.12).

The proposed discretion

A.22 Do consultees agree with our provisional view that, once the reliance principle is abandoned, the creation of a statutory discretion to decide the effect of illegality on some or all trusts is the right way forward? If consultees do not agree, do they consider that (a) future development of this area of the law should be left entirely to the courts; or (b) legislative reform should introduce a set of statutory *rules* governing the effect of illegality on some or all trusts? (paragraph 8.20).

A.23 Do consultees agree with our provisional view that the illegal trusts made subject to a statutory discretion should be limited to:[2]
(i) trusts which it would be legally wrongful to create or impose;
(ii) trusts which are created to facilitate a fraud or which arise from a transaction or arrangement with that objective;
(iii) trusts which are created to facilitate some other legal wrong or which arise from a transaction or arrangement with that objective;
(iv) trusts created in return for the commission of a legal wrong or the promise to commit a legal wrong (an "illegal consideration");
(v) trusts which expressly or necessarily require a trustee to commit a legal wrong or which tend or are intended to do so;
(vi) trusts which expressly or necessarily require a beneficiary to commit a legal wrong or which tend or are intended to do so; and
(vii) trusts which are otherwise contrary to public policy at common law?[3] (paragraph 8.40).

If consultees do not agree, please would they explain which trusts, if any, they consider should be made subject to our provisionally proposed statutory discretion. (paragraph 8.41).

A.24 Do consultees agree with our provisional view that where a statute expressly lays down what should be the consequences for a trust, of the trust involving a breach of the statute's provisions, our proposed discretion should not apply? If consultees do not agree, we ask them to explain why not. (paragraph 8.43).

---

[2] And not including "default trusts" arising on the invalidity of an express illegal trust (see para 8.23 above).

[3] Although note the doubts about the inclusion of this category which we raise in para 8.32 above.

Invalidity or unenforceability?

A.25 Do consultees agree with our provisional view that courts should have a discretion to declare an illegal trust to be invalid or valid (rather than unenforceable or enforceable)? If consultees do not agree, do they consider (a) that the courts should have a discretion to declare an illegal trust to be unenforceable or enforceable (rather than invalid or valid); or (b) that the courts should have a discretion to declare a trust to be invalid, unenforceable or valid and enforceable? (paragraph 8.49).

Structuring the discretion

A.26 Do consultees agree with our provisional view that the proposed discretion should be structured so that a court should be required to take into account specific factors in reaching its decision; and that those factors should be: (a) the seriousness of the illegality; (b) the knowledge and intention of the illegal trust beneficiary; (c) whether invalidity would tend to deter the illegality; (d) whether invalidity would further the purpose of the rule which renders the trust "illegal"; and (e) whether invalidity would be a proportionate response to the claimant's participation in the illegality? We also ask consultees whether there are any other factors which they consider the courts should take into account in exercising their proposed discretion. If consultees do not agree with our provisional views, we ask them to explain why not. (paragraph 8.63).

"Default trusts" which take effect in the event that an express illegal trust is invalid on grounds of illegality

A.27 We would be grateful for consultees' views on whether courts should have:
(a) a discretion to invalidate a default trust in favour of a person who transfers property on an illegal and invalid express trust; and/or

A.28 (b) the further discretion to order that a person who has declared him or herself trustee of an illegal and invalid express trust should transfer the trust property to the Crown. (paragraph 8.71).

A.29 Do consultees agree with our provisional view that, if there should be a discretion to invalidate a "default trust", it should be (a) a separate discretion, but (b) be structured by similar factors to those which structure our provisionally proposed discretion to invalidate an "illegal trust"? If consultees do not agree, please would they give their reasons. (paragraph 8.74).

Trustee's entitlement to property if a resulting trust, constructive trust or "default trust" trust is invalid

A.30 We would be grateful for consultees' views on whether, if a resulting trust, constructive trust or "default trust" of property in favour of a settlor (or transferor/contributor) is held to be invalid under our provisionally proposed discretion, and the property is not subject to any other express trust, the property (a) should be regarded as ownerless and fall to the Crown as *bona vacantia*; or (b) should be the trustee's by default. Further, if "trustee ownership" is preferred, how (if at all) should the windfall concern be addressed? (paragraph 8.79)

A.31   If the trustee-ownership solution is preferred, we ask consultees whether they consider that it is necessary to add, as a factor to be taken into account in exercising the court's discretion, that invalidity would unjustly enrich the trustee. (paragraph 8.82).

The starting point of the discretion

A.32   We ask consultees whether they consider that the starting point of the provisionally proposed discretion should be:
(a) validity;
(b) invalidity; or
(c) one which varies according to the form of illegal trust in question?

A.33   Alternatively we ask consultees whether they consider that it would be preferable to express no starting point. (paragraph 8.85).

A discretion to make an award on terms that the beneficiary makes a payment or transfers property to a third party

A.34   Do consultees consider that the courts should be given a discretionary power to recognise the validity of an illegal trust only on terms that require the trust beneficiary to make a payment or transfer property to a person (such as the State) who is not a party to the action? If so, we ask consultees on what basis they consider such an award should be made. (paragraph 8.88).

The interaction of the provisionally proposed discretion and the equitable maxim "he who comes to equity must come with clean hands"

A.35   Do consultees agree with our provisional view that the equitable "clean hands" maxim should have no role to play in cases which fall within the sphere of operation of our proposed discretion? If consultees do not agree, how do they consider the maxim should interrelate to our proposed discretion? (paragraph 8.91).

The effect of the invalidity of the illegal trust in relation to acts carried out pursuant to the trust

A.36   Do consultees agree with our provisional view that section 61 of the Trustee Act 1925 could provide an appropriate level of protection for trustees of illegal trusts? If consultees do not agree, what additional protections do they consider are necessary? (paragraph 8.100).

A.37   Do consultees agree that a person who received property which was held on illegal trust, from the trustee of such a trust, and where the property was owned by another in equity, should not be dealt with under our proposed statutory discretion but:- (a) should only receive such title as he or she would receive under general principles; and (b) should be liable to restitutionary claims in respect of his or her receipt in accordance with general principles? (paragraph 8.107).

A.38   Do consultees agree with our provisional conclusion that the rights and liabilities of third parties who acquire "illegal trust property" from the beneficiary of an illegal trust, or from someone who would be entitled to the property if an illegal trust was invalid, should not be dealt with under our provisionally proposed discretion, but should be decided in accordance with the standard principles which govern whether a third party (C) can obtain from another (B) a superior equitable title to property to which another person (A) was previously entitled in equity, and whether C is liable to restitutionary (or other) claims? (paragraph 8.114).

A.39 Do consultees consider that there might be any circumstances in which it would be appropriate for the court to have a discretion to recognise the third party's (C's) title subject to terms? (paragraph 8.1115).

Severance

A.40 Do consultees agree with our provisional view that where (under general principles) it is possible to sever the term(s) tainted by illegality from the trust, leaving the remaining terms of the trust valid, our provisionally proposed discretion should not apply? If consultees do not agree, please would they explain why not. (paragraph 8.116).

A.41 Do consultees agree with our provisional view that if a condition precedent is invalid because of illegality, the interest to which it is attached should take effect free of the condition, unless it is probable in all the circumstances that the settlor or testator did or would have preferred the interest to fail if the condition was invalid? (paragraph 8.124).

A.42 If consultees do not agree, would they prefer a rule whereby the interest will (a) always fail, (b) always take effect, or (c) fail unless it is probable in all the circumstances that the settlor or testator did or would have preferred the interest to take effect if the condition was invalid? (paragraph 8.125).

Illegal transactions that are neither contracts nor trusts

A.43 We ask consultees whether the same discretionary approach which we have provisionally proposed should govern the effect of illegality on contracts and trusts should also apply to govern the effect of illegality on other types of illegal transactions. We would also be grateful for consultees' help in identifying the range of illegal transactions that are neither contracts nor trusts. (paragraph 8.131).

(4) Question from Part I

Compatibility of our provisional proposals with the European Convention on Human Rights

A.44 We would be very grateful if consultees with the relevant expertise could let us know whether they agree with our view that our provisional recommendations do not infringe the European Convention for the Protection of Human Rights and Fundamental Freedoms, and, if they do not agree, to explain their reasoning. (paragraph 1.23)

APPENDIX B
SELECT BIBLIOGRAPHY

There is a large volume of published material on the subject of the illegality doctrine. The following (non-exhaustive) list identifies the main sources and other relevant materials that we have consulted during the course of writing this paper.

LAW COMMISSION PUBLICATIONS

Illegal Transactions: the Effect of Illegality on Contracts and Trusts (1999) Consultation Paper No 154.

Aggravated, Exemplary and Restitutionary Damages (1997) Law Com No 247.

BOOKS

C von Bar, *The Common European Law of Torts: Volume 2* (2000).

P Birks (ed), *English Private Law* (2000).

M Brazier and J Murphy, *Street on Torts* (10th ed 1999).

R A Buckley (ed), *Legal Structures* (1996).

R A Buckley, *The Modern Law of Negligence* (3rd ed 1999).

P Cane, *Atiyah's Accidents, Compensation and the Law* (6th ed 1999).

Charlesworth and Percy on Negligence (9th ed 1997).

Chitty on Contracts (28th ed 1999).

R Clayton and H Tomlinson, *The Law of Human Rights* (2000) Volume 1.

Clerk and Lindsell on Torts (18th ed 2000).

P Craig, *Administrative Law* (4th ed 1999).

N Enonchong, *Illegal Transactions* (1998).

W van Gerven, *Cases, Material and Text on National, Supranational and International Tort Law* (2000).

R V F Heuston and R A Buckley, *Salmond & Heuston on the Law of Torts* (21st ed 1996).

P Jaffey, *The Nature and Scope of Restitution* (2000).

M A Jones, *Textbook on Torts* (7th ed 2000).

H Kötz, *European Contract Law* (1997) Volume 1.

Lord Lester of Herne Hill and D Pannick (ed), *Human Rights Law and Practice* (1999).

A Linden, *Canadian Tort Law* (6th ed 1998).

B S Markesinis and S F Deakin, *Tort Law* (4th ed 1999).

D Miers, *State Compensation for Criminal Injuries* (1997).

The Laws of Scotland, Stair Memorial Encyclopaedia (1996) Volume 15.

K M Stanton, *The Modern Law of Tort* (1994).

F Trindade and P Cane, *The Law of Torts in Australia* (2nd ed 1993).

W V H Rogers, *Winfield and Jolowicz on Tort* (15th ed 1998).

H W R Wade and C F Forsyth, *Administrative Law* (8th ed 2000).

K Zweigert and H Kötz, *Introduction to Comparative Law* (3rd ed 1998).

ARTICLES, COMMENTS AND NOTES

J Adams and R Brownsword, "The Unfair Contract Terms Act: A Decade of Discretion" (1988) 104 LQR 94.

E K Banakas, "Tort Damages and the Decline of Fault Liability: Plato overruled, but full marks to Aristotle!" [1985] CLJ 195.

G Bosmans and F Lewis, "Proximity and Illegality in Negligence" [1992] Monash LR 237.

R A Buckley, "Illegal Transactions: Chaos or Discretion?" (2000) LS 155.

B Childs, "Of Pitts and Pendulums - A Modern Horror Story" [1991] NILQ 381.

C Debattista, "*Ex turpi causa* returns to the English Law of Torts: Taking Advantage of a wrong way out" [1984] Anglo-Am LR 15.

N Enonchong, "Effects of Illegality: A Comparative Study in French and English Law" [1995] ICLQ 196.

N Enonchong, "Illegal Transactions: The Future?" [2000] RLR 82.

W J Ford, "Tort and Illegality: The *Ex Turpi Causa* Defence in Negligence Law" (1977-78) 11 Melbourne ULR 32.

M Fordham, "The Role of *Ex Turpi Causa* in Tort Law" [1998] SJLS 238.

G H L Fridman, "The Wrongdoing Plaintiff" (1972) 18 McGill LJ 275.

S Ginsbourg and B Newton, "*Gala v Preston*: The Defence of Illegality to an Action in Negligence" [1992] Monash LR 243.

R Glofcheski, "Plaintiff's Illegality as a Bar to Recovery of Personal Injury Damages" (1999) 19 LS 6.

T Hervey, "Caveat Criminalis" (1981) 97 LQR 537.

L Klar, Case Comment [1993] Can BR 553.

R Kostal, "Currents in the Counter-Reformation: Illegality and Duty of Care in Canada and Australia" [1995] Tort LR 100.

B MacDougall, "*Ex turpi causa*: Should a Defence arise from a Base Cause?" (1991) 55 Sask LR 1.

M McInnes, "*Ex Turpi Causa* and Tort - A Canadian Perspective" [1993] CLJ 379.

R S Miller, "An Analysis and Critique of the 1992 Changes to the New Zealand Accident Compensation Scheme" (1992) 5 Canterbury LR 1.

M Noble, "Park over the border" (1996) 146 NLJ 604.

B Rodger, "*Ex Turpi*: A Location-driven Defence?" [1998] Jur Rev 201.

J Shand, "Unblinkering the Unruly Horse: Public Policy in the Law of Contract" [1972A] CLJ 144.

J R Spencer, "Ask for it, get it and sue for it - Provocation and Contributory Negligence" [1977] CLJ 242.

J Swanton, "Plaintiff a Wrongdoer: Joint Complicity in an Illegal Enterprise as a Defence to Negligence" (1981) 9 Sydney LR 304.

C G S Tan, "*Volenti non fit injuria*: An Alternative Framework" [1995] Tort LR 208.

J Wade, "Benefits Obtained Under Illegal Transactions - Reasons For and Against Allowing Restitution" (1946) 25 Texas LR 31.

E J Weinrib, "Illegality as a Tort Defence" (1976) 26 UTLJ 28.

G Williams, "Contributory Negligence and Vicarious Liability" (1954) 17 MLR 365.

K Williams, "Defences for Drunken Drivers: Public Policy on the Roads and in the Air" (1991) 54 MLR 745.